WORLD BANK WORKING PAPER NO. 194

Migrant Remittance Flows

Findings from a Global Survey of Central Banks

Jacqueline Irving
Sanket Mohapatra
Dilip Ratha

D0613382

THE WORLD BANK
Washington, D.C.

World Bank Working Papers are published to communicate the results of the Bank's work to the development community with the least possible delay. The manuscript of this paper therefore has not been prepared in accordance with the procedures appropriate to formally-edited texts. Some sources cited in this paper may be informal documents that are not readily available.

The findings, interpretations, and conclusions expressed herein are those of the author(s) and do not necessarily reflect the views of the International Bank for Reconstruction and Development/The World Bank and its affiliated organizations, or those of the Executive Directors of The World Bank or the governments they represent.

The World Bank does not guarantee the accuracy of the data included in this work. The boundaries, colors, denominations, and other information shown on any map in this work do not imply any judgment on the part of The World Bank of the legal status of any territory or the endorsement or acceptance of such boundaries.

The material in this publication is copyrighted. Copying and/or transmitting portions or all of this work without permission may be a violation of applicable law. The International Bank for Reconstruction and Development/The World Bank encourages dissemination of its work and will normally grant permission promptly to reproduce portions of the work.

For permission to photocopy or reprint any part of this work, please send a request with complete information to the Copyright Clearance Center, Inc., 222 Rosewood Drive, Danvers, MA 01923, USA, Tel: 978-750-8400, Fax: 978-750-4470, www.copyright.com.

All other queries on rights and licenses, including subsidiary rights, should be addressed to the Office of the Publisher, The World Bank, 1818 H Street NW, Washington, DC 20433, USA, Fax: 202-522-2422, email: pubrights@worldbank.org.

ISBN: 978-0-8213-8360-5
eISBN: 978-0-8213-8362-9
ISSN: 1726-5878   DOI: 10.1596/978-0-8213-8360-5

Library of Congress Cataloging-in-Publication Data has been requested.

Contents

Boxes

Abstract

Drawing on the findings from responses to a survey conducted in 2008–09 from 114 central banks worldwide (of which 33 are in Africa), this paper aims to better understand how central banks and other national institutions regulate and collect data and other information on cross-border remittance flows. Findings indicate that, although the vast majority of countries, in both sending and receiving countries, collect data on remittances, and 43 percent of receiving countries estimate informal remittances, there is a need for more frequent and better coordinated data collection, both across national institutions and among different divisions within the same national institution, as well as between countries. Survey results also indicate that many new market entrants' transfer activities are unregulated. Countries must take into account new channels and technologies, such as mobile phone service providers, in monitoring remittance flows. It will be important for national regulatory authorities to work closely with mobile telecoms network operators to strike the right regulatory balance, to better understand these new channels' associated risks and fully tap their potential for fostering inexpensive, efficient remittance transfer services. The high cost of transfers was cited in the survey as the top factor inhibiting migrants from using formal channels. Many countries, particularly in Africa, have made progress in rendering exclusivity contracts illegal, which can help increase competitiveness and reduce transfer costs. Further policy reforms and initiatives are needed to address the high costs of remittances.

Foreword

Migrant remittances provide the most tangible link between migration and development, having significant potential to reduce poverty and positively affect socioeconomic development. Drawing on the findings from a worldwide survey of central banks conducted in 2008–09, this paper aims to gain a better understanding of national regulatory environments for cross-border remittance flows and how central banks collect data and other information on remittances.

Survey findings draw attention to the need for better coordination in data collection, both across national institutions and among different divisions within the same institution in a number of countries. More systematic and frequent data monitoring will allow policy makers to make better informed and more appropriate policy responses.

As new agents, such as mobile phone service providers, enter remittance markets, countries will have to start monitoring new channels for remittance flows. The survey findings also underscore the need to reduce the still-high cost of transfers in many remittance corridors, particularly for remittances sent to Africa, including by pursuing policy reforms and initiatives that encourage more entrants to remittance markets and more competitive market conditions.

This paper is part of a broader effort of the Development Prospects Group of the World Bank to monitor and analyze migration and remittances from a development perspective.

Hans Timmer
Director
Development Prospects Group
The World Bank

Acknowledgments

We like to extend our gratitude to the central bank officials in the countries that participated in the survey for their valuable input and help with this project. We would also like to thank our World Bank colleagues in over 70 countries for their collaboration in implementing the survey. Hans Timmer, Shanta Devarajan, Louis Kasekende, and Sudhir Shetty provided guidance and encouragement. Massimo Cirasino, Neil Fantom, Michael Fuchs, Angelie Kumar, Latifah Merican, Jaya Mohanty, Joana Pascual, Rita Ramalho, Jens Reinke, and Gregory Watson provided useful comments on early versions of the survey questionnaire and advice on implementing the survey. Colleagues at the IMF African Department were helpful in directing us to the appropriate contacts at African central banks. Thanks to our colleagues in the Migration and Remittances Team, Ani Rudra Silwal, Farai Jena, Hazel Macadangdang, George Joseph, Neil Ruiz, Rebecca Russ, Sonia Plaza, and Zhimei Xu, for help in preparing data for analysis, for help in organizing a consultation meeting on the sidelines of the IMF-World Bank Annual Meeting in October 2008, and for reviewing completed surveys. We would also like to gratefully acknowledge financial support for this study from the joint African Development Bank-World Bank Africa Migration Project and G-8 Global Remittances Working Group.

Acronyms and Abbreviations

AML-CFT	Anti-money laundering-countering the financing of terrorism
BPM5	IMF's Balance of Payments and International Investment Position Manual, fifth edition
BPM6	IMF's Balance of Payments and International Investment Position Manual, sixth edition
EU	European Union
GDP	Gross domestic product
IMF	International Monetary Fund
MTO	Money transfer operator
RSP	Remittance service provider

CHAPTER 1

Introduction and Main Findings

Migrant remittances provide the most tangible and perhaps the least controversial link between migration and development, having the potential to contribute significantly to poverty reduction and achievement of other UN Millennium Development Goals. Recorded migrant remittances received by developing countries reached an estimated $338 billion in 2008, up nearly 17 percent from $289 billion in 2007.[1] The true size of migrant remittances including unrecorded flows through formal and informal channels is even higher, making remittances the largest source of external finance for many developing countries, especially poor countries. Maximizing the development impact of remittances has been recognized at the highest international policy levels, with the final declaration of the July 2009 Group of Eight Summit stating an aim to make remittance services cheaper and more accessible to migrants and their families.

This paper presents findings from a worldwide survey of central banks on cross-border migrant remittance flows. The main aims of the survey were to gain a better understanding of the regulatory environment for cross-border remittance flows and how central banks collect data and other information on migrant remittances.

Survey questionnaires were e-mailed to central banks and other national institutions in 176 countries worldwide. Two main versions of the questionnaire were developed (see appendices 1 and 2). Version 1 of the survey focuses on remittance inflows and was sent to 126 countries considered net remittance-receiving countries; version 2 focuses on remittance outflows and was sent to 50 countries considered net remittance-sending countries (see appendix 3). A version 3 survey (containing additional questions on remittance outflows) was also sent along with version 1 of the survey to several countries that send as well as receive significant amounts of remittances.[2] The survey questionnaires were an adaptation and significant extension of a World Bank survey conducted with central banks in 40 countries in 2004.[3] The survey was distributed between March and May 2008, initially to central banks in 52 African countries. By December 2009, survey submissions had been received from 114 countries (33 of which are African countries), for a response rate of 65 percent overall and 63 percent for Africa. The 112 surveys submitted in sufficiently complete form are analyzed in this paper (of which 77 surveys are from remittance-receiving countries and 35 surveys are from remittance-source countries).

The main findings of the survey are as follows:

■ There is an apparent lack of coordination on data collection and in other areas among various divisions within many individual central banks, among national institutions within a given country, and among counterpart national institutions, including for some major remittance corridors.

- As many as 43 percent of the remittance-receiving countries collect data or information on cross-border migrant remittance flows transferred through informal channels. But only 17 percent of central banks in remittance-receiving countries provided estimates of informal flows in their survey responses. Use of household and/or migrant surveys was the most cited method for estimating informal flows.

- High cost is perceived as the top single factor inhibiting migrants from using formal channels for remittance transfers. A large majority of survey respondents also cited factors that, taken together, indicate mistrust of or lack of information about financial systems, products, and channels.

- A majority of central banks cite better statistics and studies on migration and remittances as the most important areas in need of attention to improve the efficiency and security of remittance transfers. In Sub-Saharan Africa, nearly 80 percent of central banks cited better statistics and studies on migration and remittances as the most important areas needing attention.

- Anti-money laundering and combating the financing of terrorism (AML-CFT) appears to be a high priority for countries participating in the survey, many of which have recently or are currently putting in place institutional frameworks and regulations intended to better monitor suspicious cross-border transactions. Despite this, there seems to be a lack of clarity in the actual application and enforcement of AML-CFT regulations for remittance service providers (RSPs).

The survey also revealed that migrant remittance inflows have been monitored for a longer time, and in general are better monitored, than remittance outflows. In several countries, there are large discrepancies in data reporting by different agencies. Although central banks are beginning to pay attention to new technologies and alternative channels in recording remittance transactions, new entrants to the market, such as mobile phone service providers, are not yet very active in cross-border remittance transfers. Only four remittance-receiving countries reported the use of mobile phones in cross-border remittance transfers at the time of the survey.

Remittance services provided by many of the newer market entrants tend to be unregulated. However, even remittance transfer activities of as many as 6 percent of the commercial banks providing these services in remittance-receiving countries and 11 percent of the commercial banks providing these services in remittance-sending countries are not subject to any supervisory authority.

The existence of a legal requirement that money transfer operators (MTOs) partner with banks is associated with high remittance costs in remittance-receiving countries. This relationship is more pronounced in Sub-Saharan Africa. Remittance costs also tend to be higher in countries where it is compulsory to convert remittance proceeds into local currency.

Policy Implications

The results of the survey suggest that central banks and other national institutions responsible for data collection need to improve coordination in this area, with more systematic data and information exchange, better communication, and more effective division of labor to avoid duplication of efforts. Better coordination in data collection needs to occur both across institutions and among different divisions within the same institution in a number of countries.

It will be important for central banks and other national authorities responsible for remittances data collection and monitoring to give more attention to these activities, including by monitoring cross-border remittance flows data at higher frequencies and disaggregating by source country, where possible. For many remittance-receiving countries, it will also be important to revise data compilation methods to better distinguish remittance inflows from other capital inflows and to disaggregate by remittance category. Such improvements to data collection practices could be critical to effectively monitoring these cross-border flows, in the face of heightened concerns that the global financial crisis is negatively affecting the amount of cross-border migrant remittance flows to many remittance-receiving countries.

As new RSP entrants to the market emerge (for example, mobile phone service providers), it will become increasingly important for countries to take into account new channels and technologies in collecting data on and monitoring remittances. Given that the remittance transfer activities of many of the newer market entrants are not yet regulated in a number of countries,[4] national financial market regulatory authorities and mobile phone service network operators need to coordinate to strike the right balance in regulating these new technologies for money transfers.

For many remittance corridors worldwide, appropriate national policies and initiatives should be implemented to address the high cost of remittance transfers. Policies that promote competition in the remittances market can reduce transfer costs and improve service quality.[5] Discouraging exclusivity contracts between RSPs and national post offices or banks will be important for increasing competition and reducing transfer costs. Another key step toward reducing the cost of remittance transfers will be financial literacy campaigns, which can increase public awareness of remittance methods and the associated prices, putting pressure on providers to reduce costs. Promotional efforts that increase the public's trust in banks and other RSPs, backed, of course, by national policies and regulatory frameworks that promote a healthy, well-functioning, and efficient banking and financial sector, could also promote competition in the remittances market and ultimately reduce costs.

Notes

[1] For information on and analysis of the magnitude and characteristics of migrant remittance flows by region, see Ratha, Mohapatra, and Silwal (November 2009).

[2] Three countries' central banks completed the version 3 appendix questionnaire: central banks in Cyprus, The Czech Republic, and Lebanon.

[3] See de Luna Martinez (2005).

[4] Although mobile phone service providers, in particular, were reportedly providing cross-border remittance transfer services for only four remittance-receiving countries (Brazil, Indonesia,

Mexico, and the Philippines) at the time of the survey, there is growing anecdotal evidence that mobile phone service providers are becoming increasingly active in transmitting remittances domestically in many developing countries.

[5] See, for example, Ratha and Riedberg (2005).

CHAPTER 2

Findings from the Survey

Data Collection and Recording of Migrant Remittances

Migrant remittance inflows are better monitored than migrant remittance outflows and recording of inflows has occurred for a longer time.[1]

There is no regular data collection on migrant remittance inflows in only one surveyed remittance-receiving country (table 2.1).[2] This stands in marked contrast to remittance-sending countries, where 11 percent of the central banks and other national institutions surveyed indicated that there is no regular collection of data on migrant remittance outflows.[3]

There are a few probable explanations for the differing priority given to collection of data on migrant cross-border remittance flows in remittance-sending versus remittance-receiving countries. Because remittance outflows tend to be small relative to gross domestic product (GDP) in remittance-sending countries and comprise a relatively small proportion of these countries' balance of payments statistics, monitoring remittance outflows data also tends to be a relatively low priority. This could also reflect the fact that banks in European Union (EU) member countries (which comprise 16 out of the 35 remittance-source countries that responded to the survey) are not obliged to report cross-border transactions below €12,500—a threshold far higher than the amounts typically sent by migrants.[4] On the other hand, the effects of the EU thresholds have reportedly been somewhat mixed across member countries, with at least one participating EU country having found that these high reporting thresholds have had the opposite effect—motivating recent stepped up efforts to improve methods for compiling data on remittances.[5]

Notably, in a number of remittance-receiving countries, including the Philippines and Rwanda, MTOs do not report data and other information on remittance transfers directly to the central bank or any other national institution. The main source of remittances data in most countries is the periodic (ranging from daily to quarterly) reports submitted by commercial banks. In a number of cases, central banks indicated that MTOs' remittances data are captured indirectly, in the reporting by banks with which they operate in partnership. Thus, it is likely that data and information specifically on MTOs' cross-border remittance transfers may be collected more extensively (albeit indirectly) than was indicated in the survey.

Table 2.1. Migrant Remittance Inflows Are Better Monitored than Outflows

	Remittance-receiving countries (%)	Remittance-sending countries (%)
No regular data collection	1	11
Not indicated	3	3
Central banks	95	66
of which:		
Central bank only	74	51
Central bank and finance ministry	1	3
Central bank and national statistical office	17	9
Central bank and other national institution	3	3
National statistical office only[a]	0	17
Other national institutions	1	3

Source: Authors' calculations base on survey responses.

Note: Table data cover the 77 remittance-receiving countries that had responded to version 1 of the survey and the 35 remittance-sending countries that had responded to version 2 of the survey as of December 2009.

a. In 17 percent of remittance-receiving countries and 9 percent of remittance-sending countries, both national statistical offices and central banks collect these data.

Data collection by remittance-receiving countries has been occurring for longer than by remittance-sending countries. Nearly three-quarters of remittance-receiving countries reported that collection of migrant remittances data began more than five years ago, with 56 percent of the countries beginning collection of these data more than 11 years ago. In contrast, for remittance-sending countries, the corresponding figures are lower: 60 percent and 51 percent, respectively.

As many as 43 percent of respondents in remittance-receiving countries indicated that they collect information on cross-border migrant remittance flows transferred through informal channels.[6] Seventy percent of these countries collect such data with some regularity, with the most common frequencies for collecting data and information on remittances sent through informal channels being at least quarterly (cited by 24 percent; with 18 percent each citing at least monthly and at least annually).[7] Fewer than 17 percent of central banks in remittance-receiving countries provided estimates of informal flows in the survey responses, however. And only two countries completing version 2 of the questionnaire focusing on remittance outflows (Germany and the Russian Federation) indicated that they collect information on cross-border migrant remittance flows transferred through informal channels. Among those countries that send as well as receive significant amounts of remittances (and thus completed versions 1 and 3 of the questionnaire), the Czech National Bank indicated that it estimates data on remittances transferred through informal channels (box 2.1).

Box 2.1. Data Collection Practices of Countries that are Both Remittance-source and Remittance-receiving: Some Examples

Among the central bank respondents in countries that send as well as receive significant amounts of remittances, three central banks, in Cyprus, The Czech Republic and Lebanon, completed both a version 1 survey questionnaire (focus on remittance inflows) and a version 3 survey questionnaire (short supplement with focus on remittance outflows). The submissions indicate that, for Cyprus and Lebanon, a relatively high priority has been given, for at least the past several years, to regular, periodic data collection by national central banks and other institutions of both remittance inflows and outflows through formal channels in these countries. These countries' central banks reported that they collect data and other information on remittance inflows and outflows regularly (monthly). This is similar to the overall results of this study, whereby the vast majority of participating countries reported that they provide for some means of regular data collection on cross-border remittance flows.

The Czech National Bank also indicated that frequent, periodic remittance data reporting had been undertaken in 2005-07, based on the use of tracking codes by banks and other RSPs for cross-border payments. As an EU member country, however, The Czech Republic has since adopted the high threshold for reporting cross-border transactions (raised from €12,500 to €50,000 with effect from 2008), which has meant that since 2008 banks are no longer obliged to use these codes and report small cross-border transactions. Data collecting and estimating responsibilities have since undergone a transition in The Czech Republic, coinciding with adoption of the EU reporting thresholds. In 2007, the Czech National Statistical Office (CZSO) assumed responsibility from the Czech National Bank for estimating cross-border remittance flows and the CZSO introduced a new methodology for preparing these estimates by working closely with the Ministry of Labour and Social Affairs and the Research Institute of Labour and Social Affairs, which compile demographic and other data on foreigners resident in The Czech Republic and Czechs employed overseas.

Only one of these three countries (Czech Republic) collects data or estimates remittances transferred through informal channels, and there were no estimates of informal flows provided in these countries' survey submissions. The Czech National Bank indicated that it does not currently have enough information to determine the main factors that lead to transfers of remittance outflows through informal channels. Although the Bank of Lebanon does not collect data on cross-border remittance flows through informal channels, it did cite a number of factors that are likely inhibiting more transfers through formal channels, including high cost (the top factor cited overall by all participants in this study), as well as lack of bank branches located near intended remittance beneficiaries overseas, remittance senders' lack of access to bank accounts, mistrust or lack of information about electronic transfers, and remittance recipient countries' tax policies on inflows.

The most commonly cited method in remittance-receiving countries for estimating informal remittances was propensity to remit and estimates based on data and information collected from household and/or overseas migrant surveys. This method was cited by 42 percent of those central banks in countries where remittances through informal channels are estimated (figure 2.1).[8] Estimating the share of remittances in overall foreign exchange transaction volumes, including through surveys, was the next most commonly cited method in remittance-receiving countries for estimating informal remittances (24 percent). In Rwanda, for example, remittance transfers through informal channels (hand-carried and other means not reported by the banks or money transfer operators) have been estimated based on information generated from surveys that try to determine the origin of currency sold at exchange bureaus by Rwandan residents (that is, the share of currency exchanged that originates from the diaspora), which is then multiplied by the volume of monthly purchases by the exchange bureaus. Various other methods reportedly are used in these countries to estimate remittances transferred through informal channels, with sources including foreign exchange bureaus, labor ministries, foreign embassies, and, in one country's case, information published in newspapers.

Figure 2.1. Data and Information Collected from Household and/or Overseas Migrant Surveys is the Top-Cited Method for Estimating Remittance Transfers through Informal Channels

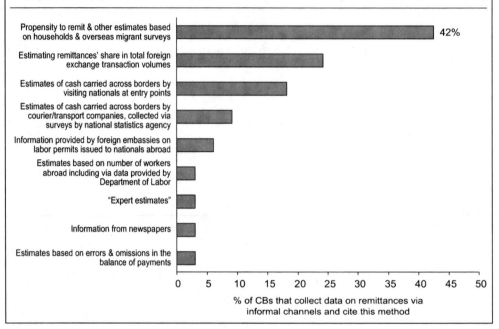

Source: Authors' calculations based on survey responses.
Note: Figure data cover the 33 remittance-receiving countries that responded positively to question 24 that data and other information on remittances transferred through informal channels are collected.

There can be a large discrepancy between what central banks reported in the survey and what they reported in their balance of payments statistics to the International Monetary Fund.[9] A comparison of remittance data reported in the survey and data reported in the World Bank's Migration and Remittances Factbook 2008, which are compiled from various issues of the IMF Balance of Payments Statistics Yearbook, reveal sizeable discrepancies for both remittance inflows and outflows for several countries (figure 2.2). For example, in the case of Ghana, remittance inflows reported to the IMF for 2007 were $105 million, while the figure reported in the survey was $1.8 billion—some 18 times as large. Figures reported in the survey for Madagascar were 15 times as large as those reported in the IMF statistics and for Rwanda, double.[10] Similarly large discrepancies between data reported in the survey and data reported in the IMF statistics were seen for Ethiopia, Lithuania, and Sierra Leone. Official figures for the latter countries, however, have been revised upward in the past several months, and are now broadly consistent with those reported in the survey.[11]

Similar, but smaller, discrepancies were observed for the countries that responded to the version 2 of the questionnaire (focus on remittance outflows), except for the United Kingdom.[12] The figure reported by the United Kingdom for remittance outflows in the survey was three times that reported in the IMF's balance of payments statistics. Some major source countries for remittances, such as Saudi Arabia, do not report any remittance data in their balance of payments reporting to the IMF.

Figure 2.2. There Is a Large Discrepancy between Remittance Data Reported in Surveys and Those Compiled from IMF Balance of Payments Statistics for Some Countries

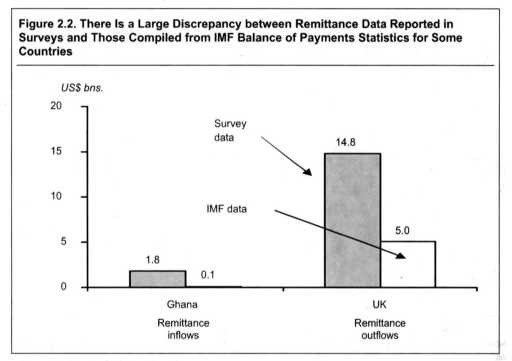

Source: Authors' calculations based on survey responses.

Note: Migrants' remittances were defined in 2008 for the purpose of the survey, in line with the IMF's *Balance of Payments and International Investment Position Manual fifth edition (BPM5)*, as the sum of workers' remittances, compensation of employees, and migrants' transfers.[13] Under the sixth edition of the *Balance of Payments and International Investment Position Manual (BPM6)*, released in mid 2009, definitions and concepts related to remittances in the balance of payments framework have been revised.[14] One of the main changes introduced by BPM6 is the replacement of the workers' remittances standard component with personal transfers, which covers all current transfers sent by individuals to individuals and thus is defined independently of the source of income of the sender and purpose of the transfer. BPM6 also includes as remittances in cash and in kind philanthropic contributions from nonprofit institutions sent from one economy to another.

A possible reason for these discrepancies is that the data collected by central banks sometimes do not allow them to distinguish migrant remittances from other small-value payments, such as cross-border trade or investment flows by nonresidents. Another reason is that central banks earlier relied on data reported solely by commercial banks, while they are now making efforts to include transfers through money transfer agencies and other providers of remittance services. Moreover, several central banks are now starting to use surveys of migrants in the destination countries and migrant household surveys in the origin countries to supplement the data reported by providers of remittance services.

Central banks are beginning to pay attention to new technologies and alternative channels when recording remittance transactions (table 2.2).[15] Transactions recorded as migrant remittance inflows are typically those through banks, money transfer operators, and post offices. However, some central banks are beginning to record transactions through new technologies such as debit or prepaid cards used at retail stores (Belarus, Cyprus, El Salvador, Guatemala, Indonesia, Morocco, Nicaragua, Poland, and Uganda), transfers through mobile phone (Indonesia, Mexico, and the Philippines), and even purchases of homes by migrants for beneficiaries (Belarus, Burkina Faso, Colombia, Cyprus, Indonesia, Moldova, Niger, the Philippines, and Tunisia).

Table 2.2. Central Banks Are Starting to Record Transfers through New Remittance Technologies and Channels

	Percent of central banks recording data as remittance transfers
Remittances through money transfer companies*	70
Electronic fund transfers through correspondent banks*	69
International money orders through post offices	47
International money orders sent electronically*	45
Bank drafts*	42
Checks issued by banks abroad*	30
Prepaid and debit cards**	29
Electronic transfer of remittances to the mobile phone**	5

Source: Authors' calculations based on survey responses.
Note: Table data cover the 77 remittance-receiving countries that responded to version 1 of the survey by December 2009.
* Banks involved. ** New technologies.

Some central banks also record transactions other than the categories in table 2.2 as migrant remittances. For example, India's central bank records local withdrawals or redemptions from nonresident deposits, gold and silver brought through passengers' baggage, and personal gifts or donations to charitable and religious institutions. The Jamaican and Samoan central banks record some portion of foreign currency received from nonresidents and converted into local currency at commercial banks, and the Moroccan central bank records travelers' checks.

Regulation and Supervision of Remittance Transfers

Supervision of cross-border remittances varies considerably across remittance services providers.[16] New entrants to the market, such as mobile money transfer service providers, are reportedly not yet very active in transferring cross-border remittance flows. Mobile phone service providers handled cross-border transactions in only four remittance-receiving countries (Brazil, Indonesia, Mexico, and the Philippines) at the time of the survey and in four (11 percent of) remittance-sending countries. Anecdotal evidence suggests, however, that these new types of RSPs are becoming increasingly active in domestic remittance transfers in many developing countries. In remittance-receiving countries, banks are the most common type of RSP involved in transferring cross-border remittances, followed by money transfer operators, post offices, and exchange bureaus (table 2.3). In remittance-sending countries, banks are also the most common providers of cross-border remittance services, closely followed by money transfer operators, with exchange bureaus ranking third.

Table 2.3. Many Remittance Services Providers (Particularly Newer Entrants) Are Not Supervised

	Remittance-receiving countries			Remittance-sending countries		
	Number of countries where these RSPs operate (a)	Number of countries where these RSPs are supervised (b)	Percent of countries (in column a) where these RSPs are supervised (c)=(b)÷(a)	Number of countries where these RSPs operate (d)	Number of countries where these RSPs are supervised (e)	Percent of countries (in column d) where these RSPs are supervised (f)=(e)÷(d)
Commercial banks	62	58	94	18	16	89
Money transfer operators	51	39	76	17	16	94
Post offices	35	22	63	9	8	89
Exchange bureaus	14	13	93	11	10	91
Credit unions, savings cooperatives, and savings and loan institutions	13	11	85	9	8	89
Microfinance institutions	9	6	67	0	0	0
Mobile phone service providers	4	3	75	4	3	75
Other financial institutions	8	8	100	3	2	67
Other nonfinancial institutions	9	7	78	3	3	100

Source: Authors' calculations based on survey responses.
Note: Table data cover the 77 remittance-receiving countries that had responded to version 1 of the survey and the 35 remittance-sending countries that had responded to version 2 of the survey by December 2009.

Not surprisingly, many of the newer market entrants' remittance services are unregulated. In 33 percent of the remittance-receiving countries where microfinance institutions operate and in one out of the four remittance-receiving countries where mobile phone service providers operate, remittance services provided by these types of institutions are not subject to any supervisory authority. There was no supervisory institution for post offices undertaking these activities in 37 percent of the remittance-receiving countries where they operate. Even the remittance services provided by commercial banks in 6 percent of remittance-receiving countries are not subject to any supervisory authority. Money transfer operators' remittance services are reportedly overseen by supervisory authorities in just over three-quarters of the remittance-receiving countries in which they operate. In an even higher proportion of remittance-sending countries, remittance outflows by banks and exchange bureaus are not supervised by any national entity.

Data collection from non-bank RSPs appears to be influenced by the requirement for partnerships with banks. Central banks are more likely to collect data from non-bank RSPs in countries that do not require a non-bank RSP to partner with a bank. MTOs and post offices in developing countries are more likely to report inflows to the central bank in countries that do not require non-bank RSPs to operate in partnerships with banks.

Anti-money laundering and combating the financing of terrorism (AML-CFT) appears to be a high priority for countries participating in the survey. In spite of this, there seems to be a lack of clarity in the application of AML-CFT regulations for RSPs in remittance-receiving and sending countries. Many central banks have recently or are currently putting in place institutional frameworks and regulations to better monitor suspicious cross-border transactions. Three-quarters of central banks in remittance-receiving countries reported being involved in developing or implementing national policies related to AML-CFT. However, the central bank enforces sanctions in just under one-third of the remittance-receiving countries, while a separate national authority specifically charged with preventing money laundering enforces sanctions in 34 percent of these countries, and the ministry of finance is involved in 19 percent of these countries. In nine (12 percent of) remittance-receiving countries, the first two institutions work together to enforce sanctions; in three of these countries, the two institutions also work together with the finance ministry. The ministry of finance is involved in enforcing anti-money-laundering sanctions in nearly one-fifth of remittance-receiving countries. Other national or regional entities involved in enforcing anti-money-laundering sanctions include the financial intelligence unit, the financial system superintendency, the criminal prosecutor, the ministry of justice and anticorruption commission, and various other judicial, anticorruption, and financial intelligence units.

In remittance-sending countries, just over half of central banks (19 out of 35) surveyed indicated that they were involved in developing or implementing AML-CFT regulations. Central banks in considerably fewer (just over one-fifth of) remittance-sending countries reported being involved in enforcing AML-CFT sanctions.[17]

In 68 percent of remittance-receiving countries, commercial banks are required to file suspicious activity reports with various national authorities, including the central bank, finance ministry, financial intelligence units, and other national agencies with responsibility for financial crimes and anti-money laundering. Commercial banks are required to file currency transaction reports in 70 percent of remittance-receiving countries. However, only 34 percent of remittance-receiving countries report requiring MTOs to file suspicious activity reports directly with national authorities. MTOs are required to file currency transaction reports in 35 percent of remittance-receiving countries. In Algeria, Rwanda, and Uganda, currency transaction reports and suspicious activity reports are filed by partner banks or banks where MTOs have accounts.

By comparison, a smaller fraction (40 percent) of surveyed remittance-sending countries report requiring commercial banks to file suspicious activity reports with national authorities, and 17 percent report requiring currency transaction reports. Thirty-four percent of remittance-sending countries require MTOs to file suspicious activity reports, according to the survey results, while 14 percent require MTOs to file currency transaction reports. Italy requires currency transaction reports from commercial banks and MTOs only when a transaction is considered suspicious.

These reporting requirements are less widely enforced for other types of RSPs (for example, post offices and microfinance institutions). Just under one-quarter of surveyed remittance-receiving countries require post offices to file suspicious activity reports, and only five countries require such reports from MFIs. For remittance-sending countries, just over one-quarter require post offices to file suspicious activity reports, and only three countries require such reports from MFIs.

These responses suggest a lack of clarity on how broader regulations related to anti-money laundering and combating the financing of terrorism (AML-CFT) are applied to specific types of remittance service providers.

Remittance Costs

The majority of central bank respondents in both remittance-receiving and -sending countries cited high cost as the top single factor inhibiting migrants from using formal channels for remittance transfers (figure 2.3).[18] After high cost, lack of a bank branch near the intended recipient, and recipients'/senders' lack of access to bank accounts, ranked as the second most cited impediments overall, although for remittance-receiving countries recipients' mistrust of and/or lack of information on electronic transfers ranked nearly as highly. For remittance-source countries, senders'/recipients' lack of valid ID ranked as highly. Notably, two-thirds of the remittance-receiving countries' central banks and 46 percent of remittance-sending countries' central banks cited factors that, taken together, indicate mistrust of and/or lack of information on and access to financial systems, products, and institutions are major factors inhibiting greater access to formal channels.

For the Sub-Saharan African countries' central banks that participated in the survey,[19] high cost was most often cited as the top factor inhibiting migrants from using formal channels for remittance transfers. Sixty-eight percent of Sub-Saharan African countries' central banks cited high cost a major inhibiting factor (figure 2.4), while absence of a bank branch near the beneficiary and recipients' lack of access to bank accounts were the second- and third-highest ranking factors (cited by 64 percent and 61 percent, respectively). Although central banks in Sub-Saharan Africa reported the same top seven factors as inhibiting the use of formal channels as did all surveyed countries, a correspondingly higher share of Sub-Saharan African respondents cited these factors, with the exception of mistrust of and/or lack of information on electronic transfers.

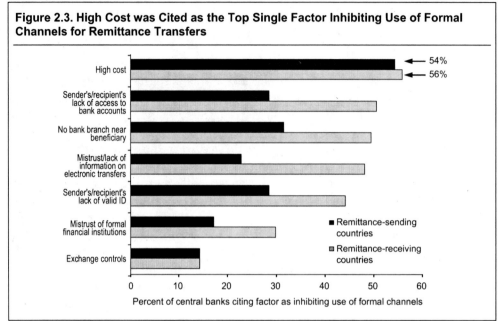

Figure 2.3. High Cost was Cited as the Top Single Factor Inhibiting Use of Formal Channels for Remittance Transfers

Source: Authors' calculations based on survey responses.

Note: Figure data cover the 77 remittance-receiving countries that had responded to version 1 of the survey and the 35 remittance-sending countries that had responded to version 2 of the survey by December 2009.

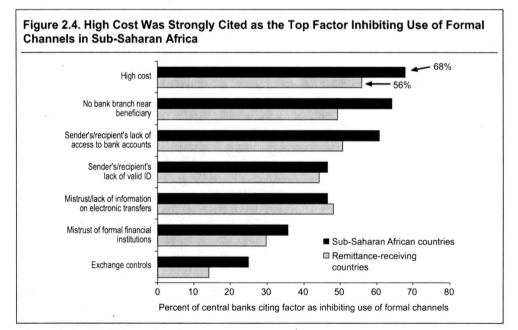

Figure 2.4. High Cost Was Strongly Cited as the Top Factor Inhibiting Use of Formal Channels in Sub-Saharan Africa

Source: Authors' calculations based on survey responses.

Note: Figure data cover the 28 Sub-Saharan African remittance-receiving countries that responded to version 1 of the survey.

Requiring MTOs and post offices to work in partnership with banks is usually associated with a perception of high remittance costs.[20] A high cost of remittance services, cited as the top factor inhibiting the use of formal channels by a majority of central banks in developing countries, appears to be related to the extent to which money transfer companies and post offices are required to operate in partnership with banks in order to receive remittance inflows.[21] Sixty-nine percent of remittance-receiving countries that require an MTO to operate in partnership with a bank cited high cost as a factor inhibiting the use of formal remittance channels, compared with 44 percent of countries that do not require such a partnership (figure 2.5).[22] With the exception of the Bahamas, Oman, Portugal, Russia, and South Africa, no remittance-sending country reported requiring MTOs to operate in a legal partnership with a bank.[23]

Figure 2.5. Requiring MTOs to Partner with Banks to Receive Remittance Inflows Is Associated with Perception of High Costs

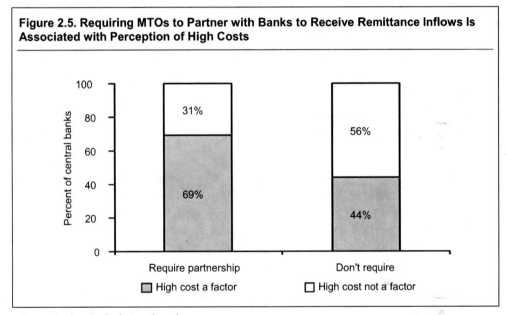

Source: Authors' calculations based on survey responses.
Note: Figure data cover the 77 remittance-receiving countries that had responded to version 1 of the survey as of December 2009.

Tighter exchange controls are also associated with the perception of high costs as a factor inhibiting the use of formal remittance channels. The share of central banks in remittance-receiving countries citing remittance costs as a factor inhibiting the use of formal remittance channels is 12 percentage points higher in those countries where the recipients are required to convert the remittances into local currency than it is in countries that do not have a similar conversion requirement (figure 2.6).[24] Not surprisingly, the survey also found that legal requirements for non-bank providers of remittance services such as money transfer agencies, exchange bureaus, and post offices to operate only in partnerships with banks are more common in countries with tighter exchange controls.

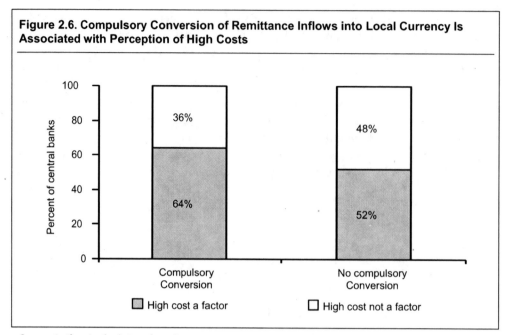

Figure 2.6. Compulsory Conversion of Remittance Inflows into Local Currency Is Associated with Perception of High Costs

Source: Authors' calculations based on survey responses.

Note: Figure data cover the 77 remittance-receiving countries that had responded to version 1 of the survey as of December 2009.

Greater freedom of money transfer agencies and post offices to operate independently of banks can increase the degree of competition in the remittance market and thereby put downward pressure on costs. Allowing a variety of well supervised and appropriately regulated RSPs to operate, and liberalizing exchange controls such as requirements for compulsory conversion of remittance inflows into local currency can encourage the use of formal remittance channels, improve competition in the remittance market, and reduce costs, ultimately benefiting the remittance receivers.

Policies to Improve Remittance Transfers

Sixty-five percent of central banks in remittance-receiving countries and 31 percent of central banks in remittance-sending countries cited better statistics and studies on migration as the area most in need of attention (figure 2.7). Better statistics on remittances was cited by a similar share of respondents in both groups (61 percent and 29 percent, respectively).[25] New technologies and products for the provision of remittances services ranked alongside the latter factor for remittance-source countries, and ranked third for remittance-receiving countries (cited by 51 percent). Delivery of remittances to remote areas was the next-highest ranking area cited for remittance-receiving countries (cited by just under half).

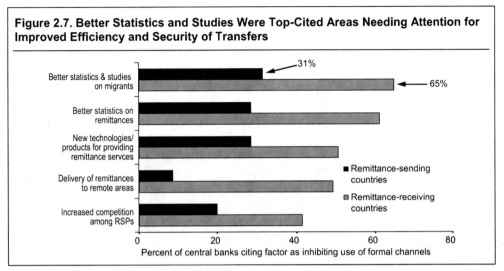

Figure 2.7. Better Statistics and Studies Were Top-Cited Areas Needing Attention for Improved Efficiency and Security of Transfers

Source: Authors' calculations based on survey responses.
Note: Figure data cover the 77 remittance-receiving countries that had responded to version 1 of the survey and the 35 remittance-sending countries that had responded to version 2 of the survey as of December 2009.

A significantly higher share of central banks in Sub-Saharan Africa (79 percent) than in remittance-receiving countries as a whole (65 percent) cited better statistics and studies on migration and better statistics on remittances as the areas most in need of attention for more efficient and secure transfer and delivery of migrant remittances (figure 2.8). Delivery of remittances to remote areas was the next-highest ranking area needing attention, cited by 64 percent of Sub-Saharan African central banks, followed by a need for increased competition among RSPs (cited by half).

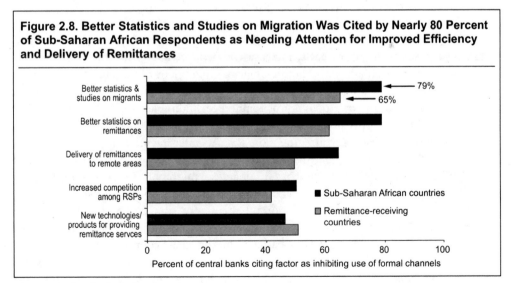

Figure 2.8. Better Statistics and Studies on Migration Was Cited by Nearly 80 Percent of Sub-Saharan African Respondents as Needing Attention for Improved Efficiency and Delivery of Remittances

Source: Authors' calculations based on survey responses.
Note: Figure data cover the 28 Sub-Saharan African remittance-receiving countries that had responded to version 1 of the survey.

Just under one-third of remittance-receiving countries indicated that there are policy initiatives planned or underway to expand the outreach of remittance services to rural areas.[26] Developing new technologies for remittance delivery—mobile phone, Internet, cash cards, ATMs—was cited by one-quarter of those indicating that they have such initiatives as the means of doing so.

Among those countries that have policy initiatives planned or underway for expanding access to remittance services in remote areas, 38 percent of respondents indicate some role for banks, whether alone or in partnership with other RSPs. Encouraging banks to expand branch networks to rural areas and plans to "bank the unbanked" together were cited by one-quarter of these respondents, while 8 percent indicated plans to encourage partnerships between banks and MTOs or non-governmental organizations to better serve rural locations.

In many remittance-receiving countries, there are also initiatives underway that provide for a larger role for non-bank RSPs. Thirteen percent of respondents in remittance-receiving countries that indicated that they have policy initiatives for expanding access to remittance services in remote areas specifically cited plans to newly allow or further encourage microfinance institutions to deliver remittances to beneficiaries.

Forty percent of central banks in remittance-receiving countries reported providing some type of incentive for migrants to transfer their money back home.[27] Thirty-six percent of central banks report providing attractive investment options, 14 percent provide tax breaks, and 10 percent[28] provide matching funds for investment projects. A few provide other types of incentives for migrants. For example, the authorities and banks in Burkina Faso have undertaken information campaigns to tap into the savings of migrants living in Côte d'Ivoire and Italy and to encourage investment in land, especially in rural and underdeveloped areas. Peru recently introduced a government financing program for real estate investment by migrants for low-income housing.

Twenty-three percent of central banks in remittance-receiving countries reported having initiatives to reduce costs, increase competition, and foster the use of formal channels. Bangladesh allows MFIs to deliver remittances in rural areas in partnership with banks. It has also introduced an Automated Clearing and Settlement System for faster, secure, and low-cost delivery of remittances. Ethiopia reported plans to allow institutions such as post offices and MFIs to offer remittance services. Sierra Leone, Uganda, and Zambia are encouraging more RSPs to enter the market.

The Albanian central bank has introduced an array of measures, including designing a communication strategy to increase migrants' awareness of banking products and transfer services, instituting bilateral agreements between domestic banks and their counterparts in important remittance source countries (Greece and Italy), and encouraging the Albanian post office to establish cooperation arrangements with post offices and postal savings banks in migrant host countries. The Philippines' central bank has undertaken measures to increase the financial literacy of overseas Filipino workers and their beneficiaries, such as holding seminars both locally in the Philippines and overseas, which complement the predeparture orientation sessions given by the Philippine Overseas Employment Administration (POEA) that include providing information on available remittance channels as well as savings and investment opportunities. In Tajikistan, where migrant remittances are a large share of GDP, the central bank's efforts are aimed at improving the public's trust in the banking system in order to increase the use of formal channels. Fiji and Moldova also have programs to boost public awareness and financial literacy campaigns.

Several remittance-source countries (26 percent) reported that they have initiatives to foster the use of formal channels in remittance transfers. Germany and New Zealand have introduced websites that provide information on available channels and costs for selected remittance corridors, which can foster transparency and the use of formal remittance channels.[29] Switzerland provides a brochure with similar information to migrants. In Spain, the government is working together with associations of banks and saving institutions to improve transparency and competition in the remittance market, reduce costs, and make it easier and cheaper to send remittances. The Norwegian authorities are considering possible changes in regulations to facilitate remittances. Russia has a public campaign underway to increase financial literacy.

Notes

[1] Results based on responses to questions 1, 13, 27, and 28 of the survey questionnaire.

[2] There is reportedly no regular data collection on remittance inflows in only one (1 percent) of the remittance-receiving countries (Malawi), although even in that country, the central bank respondents indicated that they considered collection of these data important but they lacked the resources and capacity to do so.

[3] Among remittance-sending countries where there is no regular collection of data on cross-border migrant remittance flows are Hong Kong, China; New Zealand; and Saudi Arabia (the latter country did not respond to the survey).

[4] The per-transaction reporting threshold has recently been raised even higher, to €50,000, in the national legislation of many European countries for cross-border transactions between residents in EU members and/or those of Iceland, Liechtenstein, Norway, and Switzerland.

[5] The Bank of Spain Balance of Payments Division specifically reported that the higher priority that it has been according to remittance data compilation efforts has been prompted at least partly by the higher EU reporting thresholds.

[6] Draws on the results of responses to question 24 of the survey questionnaire.

[7] According to the survey results, the most commonly cited frequency for collecting data and other information on remittance transfers through formal channels was monthly in both remittance-receiving and -source countries (cited by 64 percent and 37 percent, respectively, of those central banks and other institutions indicating that they collect data with some regularity), followed by quarterly (20 percent and 23 percent, respectively).

[8] Draws on the results of responses to question 25 of the survey questionnaire.

[9] Draws on the results of responses to question 2 of the survey questionnaire.

[10] In some countries, figures cited in press reports are significantly higher than that reported either in the balance of payments statistics or in the central bank survey. For example, in the case of Tanzania, the figure for remittance inflows cited in the press is in the range of $300 million, while that reported to the IMF and the central bank survey was $15 million.

[11] Remittance inflow figures reported to the IMF as of mid-2008 were $172 million for Ethiopia (subsequently revised up to $359 million at the time of writing this paper); $994 million for Lithuania (revised to $1,427 million); and $38 million for Sierra Leone (revised to $148 million).

[12] The discrepancy for Denmark, Finland, Germany, Greece, and Japan was in the range of 8–18 percent, likely explained by reporting lags.

[13] See IMF (1993) and World Bank (2005), respectively.

[14] See IMF (2009a).

[15] Draws on the results of responses to question 20 of the survey questionnaire.

[16] Draws on the results of responses to question 33 of the survey questionnaire.

[17] Other institutions (for example, the Financial Regulator in Ireland, Her Majesty's Revenue and Customs in the United Kingdom, and the Ministry of Finance in Italy) work in cooperation with law enforcement authorities to enforce sanctions ranging from fines, freezing of funds, withdrawal of banking license, and even imprisonment.

[18] Draws on the results of responses to question 103 of the survey questionnaire.

[19] Refers to the 28 Sub-Saharan African countries, excluding South Africa, which had completed the survey as of December 2009.

[20] Draws on the results of responses to questions 34 and 103 of the survey questionnaire.

[21] The remittance-receiving countries that reported requiring firms specializing in money transfers (such as Western Union and Moneygram) to operate in partnership with banks to receive remittance inflows are Albania, Algeria, Armenia, Azerbaijan, Bangladesh, Belarus, Brazil, Burkina Faso, Burundi, Eritrea, Ethiopia, Guinea-Bissau, Haiti, India, Lithuania, Mali, Morocco, Mozambique, Niger, Nigeria, Romania, Rwanda, Senegal, Sierra Leone, Tajikistan, Tanzania, Tunisia, Turkey, and Uganda.

[22] That is, 20 central banks—or 69 percent of the total 29 central banks in remittance-receiving countries responding to this question that do require an MTO to operate in partnership with a bank—cited high cost as a factor inhibiting the use of formal remittance channels. This compares with 11 central banks—or 44 percent of the total 25 central banks in remittance-receiving countries responding to this question that do *not* require an MTO to operate in partnership with a bank—that cited high cost as a factor inhibiting the use of formal remittance channels.

[23] Draws on the results of responses to question 34 of the survey questionnaire.

[24] Draws on the results of responses to questions 78 and 103 of the survey questionnaire. Sixteen central banks—or sixty-four percent of the total 25 central banks in remittance-receiving countries responding to this question that do require recipients to convert their remittances into local currency—cited remittance costs as a factor inhibiting the use of formal remittance channels. This compares with 27 central banks—or fifty-two percent of the total 52 central banks in remittance-receiving countries responding to this question that do *not* require recipients to convert their remittances into local currency—that cited remittance costs as a factor inhibiting the use of formal remittance channels.

[25] Draws on the results of responses to question 89 of the survey questionnaire.

[26] Draws on the results of responses to questions 86 and 87 of the survey questionnaire.

[27] Draws on the results of responses to question 105 of the survey questionnaire.

[28] These countries include Belarus, Cape Verde, El Salvador, Haiti, Honduras, Mexico, Sierra Leone, and Tunisia.

[29] The objectives are similar to those of the United Kingdom Department for International Development's sendmoneyhome.org website. New Zealand's efforts are part of a broader New Zealand-Pacific Remittance Project to reduce the average total transactional cost of remittances to less than 5 percent by increasing access to banking services and products, promoting competition, and disseminating financial capability information and education about available money transfer methods and associated costs.

CHAPTER 3

Policy Implications

Survey findings draw attention to a significant lack of coordination by many central banks in data collection, at a few different levels. Central banks and other national institutions responsible for data collection need to improve coordination in this area, with more systematic data and information exchange, better communication, and more effective division of labor to avoid duplication of efforts. Better coordination in data collection needs to occur both across institutions and among different divisions within the same institution in a number of countries.

For major remittance corridors, developing some means of regular, more systematic sharing of data and information on migrant remittance flows between counterpart national institutions is also important, in order to ensure the formulation of appropriate national policies, particularly in response to sudden and emerging changes in the size, composition, and channels for remittance transfers.

Although 96 percent of remittance-receiving countries have some regular means of data collection, a majority of central banks in the countries surveyed, and nearly 80 percent in Sub-Saharan Africa, cite a need for better statistics and studies on migration and remittances as the most important policy area for improving the efficiency and security of remittance transfers. It will be important for central banks and other national authorities responsible for data collection to give further attention to improving procedures for data collection, including by monitoring cross-border remittance flows data at higher frequencies and disaggregating by source country where possible. For many remittance-receiving countries, it will also be important to revise data compilation methods to better distinguish remittance inflows from other types of inflows and to disaggregate by remittance category. Such improvements to data collection practices will be critical to effectively monitoring these cross-border flows, particularly in the face of heightened concerns that the global financial crisis—and the ensuing economic downturns in a number of migrant destination countries—have been negatively affecting the amount of cross-border migrant remittance flows to many remittance-receiving countries. More systematic and frequent data monitoring and evaluation—backed by reporting regulations to ensure that the remittance transfer transactions of as many remittance service providers as possible are captured—could improve the ability of policy makers to develop better informed and more appropriate policy responses to changes in cross-border flows that could impact macroeconomic stability and poverty levels.[1] It will be important for countries to continue to build on the work of developing standard remittances concepts and statistical definitions that led in 2009 to the sixth edition of the IMF's Balance of Payments and International Investment Position Manual (BPM6) and the IMF's *International Transactions in*

Remittances: Guide for Compilers and Users, by continuing to exchange information and confer on developing more harmonized approaches to data reporting and compilation including, for example, thresholds for reporting remittances sent through electronic fund transfers.[2]

As new types of RSP emerge, it will become increasingly important for countries to take into account new channels and technologies in collecting data and monitoring remittances transferred through these new channels. These data and information will be key to developing appropriate national policy responses, particularly for countries where remittance inflows are significant relative to the size of the economy.

Although many of the new entrants to the RSP market are not yet very active in transferring cross-border remittances, there is significant potential for newly emerging technologies and channels, such as mobile phone service providers, to become more significant in future in cross-border remittance transfers, particularly as they are already present in some domestic remittance transfer markets. Given that the remittance transfer activities of many of the newer market entrants are not regulated at all in a number of countries, national financial market regulatory authorities and mobile phone service network operators should work closely to strike the right balance in regulating these new technologies for money transfer.[3] This would allow for better monitoring and understanding of the risks associated with these new channels, as well as reaching the full potential of these new technologies in fostering inexpensive and efficient remittance transfer services to the poor.

Developing new delivery technologies—mobile phone, Internet, cash cards—is one of the ways countries are expanding the reach of remittances services to rural areas, according to the survey results. It would be useful for countries with a large number of recipients of remittances in rural areas to exchange information and lessons learned on best practices, and share new technologies in this area.

There may be potential for certain non-bank RSPs to play a greater role in provision of remittance services to recipients in rural areas. For example, for some countries, it may make sense for national postal systems, where they have extensive rural branch networks, to adopt new technologies for remittance transfers or form partnerships with MTOs or other RSPs that have access to good telecoms infrastructure and clearing systems. In remittance-receiving countries where microfinance institutions have a known and trusted presence in rural areas, they may also play a potentially useful role in expanding the outreach of remittance delivery through formal channels to rural areas and possibly also increase the access of rural populations that are currently unbanked to remittance-linked savings and other financial products.

For many remittance corridors worldwide, appropriate national policies and initiatives should be implemented to address the high cost of remittance transfers—cited in the survey results as the top single factor inhibiting migrants from using formal channels. Policies and operating environments that facilitate the entrance of new RSPs in the market tend to lead to a reduction in transfer costs and an improvement in service quality.[4] Compared with other regions, the cost of remittance transfers through formal channels to and within Sub-Saharan Africa still tends to be quite high due largely to national regulatory frameworks that often do not encourage a competitive operating environment for RSPs.[5] Rendering it illegal for MTOs to require exclusivity contracts is one important step that has been taken recently by a number of national regulatory authorities in Africa and elsewhere. Making further progress to this end in countries where exclusivity contracts remain in effect will be important to increasing competitiveness and reducing transfer costs.

The cost of remittance services is determined by potential customers' awareness of choices, as well as the number of alternative channels and market competitors, among other factors (see Ratha and Riedberg, 2005). Thus, another step toward reducing costs of remittance transfer would be expanding financial literacy campaigns and promotional efforts that increase the public's trust in banks and other RSPs and address the lack of information on remittance products and channels. These steps could also go some way toward addressing factors cited by a large majority of survey respondents as inhibiting migrants from using formal transfer channels.

Further empirical research, taking this work forward, could focus on examining whether remittance-receiving countries are implementing policies that enable them to maximize the developmental benefits associated with remittance inflows. Further work in this area could also usefully contribute by advising on how countries might develop policies to maximize the development benefits that potentially could accrue from remittance inflows, particularly in the context of the rapidly changing channels and technologies for remittance transfer.[6]

Notes

[1] Even where revisions to data compilation methods improve the accuracy of remittance inflows and/or outflows for more recent periods in a time series, however, the comparability of remittances data across a time series may be impeded, at least for a transition period, following revision of compilation methods, where it is not possible to revise the data for earlier periods in the time series in line with the new compilation methods.

[2] See IMF (2009a) and IMF (2009b).

[3] One forum that is working with governments and development agencies to identify the optimum regulatory framework and to develop a commercial and technical framework to enable mobile phone services providers to set up mobile money transfer services is the Mobile Money Transfer program under the Groupe Speciale Mobile Association (GSMA). Further information on the work and aims of this program is available at its website: http://216.239.213.7/mmt/index.asp.

[4] See, for example, Orozco (2002) and Ratha and Riedberg (2005).

[5] See also IFAD (2007).

[6] These recommendations on how this work could be taken forward were based on comments provided by the Central Bank of the Republic of Turkey, which provided input for this paper's survey on data collection and regulation of cross-border remittance flows.

References

Bank for International Settlements and World Bank, *General Principles for International Remittance Services*, Basel, Switzerland: Bank for International Settlements, 2007.

De Luna Martinez, José. 2005. *Workers' Remittances to Developing Countries: A Survey with Central Banks on Selected Public Policy Issues*. World Bank Policy Research Working Paper No. 3638. Washington, DC: World Bank.

International Fund for Agricultural Development. 2007. *Sending Money Home: Worldwide Remittance Flows to Developing and Transition Countries*. Rome: IFAD.

International Monetary Fund. 1993. *Balance of Payments and International Investment Position Manual, Fifth Edition (BPM5)*. Washington, DC: IMF.

———. 2009a. *Balance of Payments and International Investment Position Manual, Sixth Edition (BPM6)*. Washington, DC: IMF.

———. 2009b. *International Transactions in Remittances: Guide for Compilers and Users*. Washington, DC: IMF

Orozco, Manuel. 2002. *Attracting Remittances: Market, Money and Reduced Costs*. Washington, DC: Inter-American Development Bank.

Ratha, Dilip. 2007. "Leveraging Remittances for Development." Migration Policy Institute Policy Brief.

———, and J. Riedberg. 2005. "On Reducing Remittance Costs." Washington, DC: World Bank.

———, Sanket Mohapatra, and Ani Silwal. 2009. "Migration and Development Brief 11." Washington, DC: World Bank.

World Bank. 2005. "Economic Implications of Remittances and Migration," *Global Economic Prospects*. Washington, DC: World Bank.

Appendixes

Appendix 1. Survey Questionnaire: Focus on Remittance Inflows

Introduction and Outline

Thank you for taking the time to complete our survey on the national regulatory environment for migrants' cross-border remittance flows, monitoring practices, and migrant cross-border remittances data. This survey is part of a larger cross-country data and information collection exercise intended to fill the knowledge gap on the impact of migrant remittances on development. The findings from this survey, which is being sent to central banks and other relevant national authorities worldwide, are intended to help inform future efforts to strengthen the capacity of national policy makers and institutions to analyze relevant trends and determinants of these capital flows in order to enhance their development impact.

The survey questionnaire that follows is structured in five main sections, following the outline below. Please complete all of the questions that are relevant to your country's particular situation as a recipient and/or source of remittance flows.

Section I. Recent data collected on remittance inflows

Section II. Data collection practices: Remittance inflows

Section III. National regulatory environment for migrant remittance flows

Section IV. Financial infrastructure supporting cross-border remittance flows

Section V. Best Practices, Public Policy Issues, Bilateral Agreements for Data and Technology Sharing

---

Please return the completed questionnaire to the World Bank Group, to the attention of Mr. Dilip Ratha, Manager, Migration & Remittances Team, World Bank Group, 1818 H Street, NW, Washington, DC 20433, USA, Fax +1-202-522-3564, Email: Dratha@worldbank.org

---

Name of person(s) responding to this questionnaire:

Position and Department/Division:

Institution and location (city, country):

Phone number:

Email address:

Date questionnaire completed (dd/mm/yyyy):

Are you completing this questionnaire on the behalf of another colleague(s)? If yes, please provide the name(s), position(s), department(s) and contact details for that colleague(s) below.

I. Recent Data Collected on Remittance Inflows

By compiling available national data on migrant remittance flows, responses to this set of questions will improve the understanding of the magnitude and characteristics of remittance flows, with a view to generating informed policy recommendations that would maximize their positive development impact.

1. Does your institution collect data on cross-border remittance inflows?

a. Yes	☐	
b. No, it is another institution(s): please specify:	☐	If you checked No at left, skip to Section III, Question 32

2. According to your estimates, what is the annual volume of cross-border remittance inflows to your country since 2005?

Table 1

	i. Workers' remittance inflows (US$)	ii. Compensation of employees (US$)	iii. Migrants' transfers (US$)	iv. Total (US$)	v. Informal remittance inflows (US$)
a) 2007 (forecast)					
b) 2006					
c) 2005					

Please also provide these data for earlier years if available:

d) 2004					
e) 2003					
f) 2002					

3. According to your most recently available estimates for annual remittance **inflows**, please list the top ten source countries for cross-border remittance flows to your country by ranking from 1 to 10 in Table 2 below, with a rank of 1 going to the top source country for remittance **inflows.** If data are available, please provide estimates of the amount of these annual remittance inflows by source country in the table's second column.

Table 2

i. Top source countries (List as many as possible)	ii. Estimated amount of annual remittance inflows for most recently available year (US$) Specify year:
1)	
2)	
3)	
4)	
5)	
6)	
7)	
8)	
9)	
10)	

4. For the top 10 source countries that you listed in Question 3, please briefly note below what you believe to be the main factor(s) driving remittance inflows from this country.

Table 3

i. Top source countries (List as many as possible)	ii. What are the main factor(s) driving remittance inflows from this country?
1)	
2)	
3)	
4)	
5)	
6)	
7)	
8)	
9)	
10)	

5. Would you please provide as much of the following data as are available on remittance **inflows** for each applicable transfer instrument for the most recent two-year period in Table 4? Please be sure to specify the actual year (indicating whether it is calendar or fiscal year). Please indicate the currency of denomination if other than U.S. dollars.

Table 4

Instrument to transfer cross-border remittance inflows	Year 1 (specify year:)		Year 2 (specify year:)	
	i. Number of transactions	ii. Volume of transactions (US$)	iii. Number of transactions	iv. Volume of transactions (US$)
a) Bank drafts				
b) Checks issued by banks abroad				
c) International money orders sent by post				
d) International money orders sent electronically				
e) Electronic wire via money transfer operators (for example, Money Gram, Western Union)				
f) Electronic fund transfers through correspondent banks				
g) Debit cards				
h) Pre-paid cards				
i) Money reported at airports/borders carried by relatives traveling to home country				
j) Money transfer by mobile phone				
k) Other, please specify:				
l) Total				

6. Are there particular periods of the year when remittance inflows tend to be much larger or much smaller?

a. Yes	☐	b. No	☐

7. Does your country have guest-worker programs?

a. Yes	☐	If you checked Yes at left, please go to Q. 8
b. No	☐	If you checked No at left, go to Q. 9

8. Please indicate below with which country(ies) and sector(s) of the economy these guest worker programs are in effect?

i. Country	ii. Sector
a)	
b)	
c)	
d)	

9. If applicable: During which seasons/periods of the year are remittance **inflows** likely to be larger?

10. If applicable: During which seasons/periods of the year are remittance **inflows** likely to be smaller?

11. Please complete Table 5 for each type of institution listed below that delivers remittance **inflows** to recipients in your country at present. Please provide estimates, if necessary.

Table 5

	i. Number of institutions	ii. Total number of branches	iii. Number of branches in rural areas
a) Firms specialized in money transfers (Western Union, Money Gram, etc.)			
b) Private commercial banks			
c) State-owned banks			
d) Exchange bureaus			
e) Microfinance institutions			
f) Savings and loan institutions			
g) Credit unions and savings cooperatives			
h) Other financial institutions that receive and/or send remittances: please specify			
i) Post offices			
j) Mobile phone/telecoms service providers			
k) Other non-financial institutions that deliver remittances: please specify			

II. Data Collection Practices: Remittance inflows

Effective national data collection and other systems and procedures for monitoring migrant remittance flows help enable national policy makers to devise appropriate policies that would promote the beneficial development effects of remittances. This set of questions aims to take an inventory of national data collection practices to assess national capacity in this area on a cross-country basis.

12. Which division(s) within your institution currently is(are) responsible for collecting data on remittance **inflows**?

13. How long ago did your institution first begin collecting data and information on remittance **inflows**?

a. Over the past year	☐
b. 2-5 years ago	☐
c. 6-10 years ago	☐
d. 11-20 years ago	☐
e. More than 20 years ago	☐
f. Other: please specify	☐

14. How often does your institution collect data and information on remittance **inflows**?

a. Monthly	☐
b. Quarterly	☐
c. Semi-annually	☐
d. Annually	☐
e. Occasionally	☐
f. Other: please specify	☐

15. Other than changes in data collection frequency, have your data collection practices for remittance **inflows** changed in other ways over the past five years?

a. Yes	☐	
b. No	☐	If you checked No at left, skip to Q. 17

16. Please indicate the ways in which these practices have changed. Check all that apply.

a. In terms of types of data compiled	☐	Please specify how:	
b. In terms of changes in sources of data	☐	Please specify how:	
c. Other	☐	Please specify:	

17. Do you have any plans to change the coverage of your data on remittances **inflows** and/or the methodology used to measure remittances?

a. Yes	☐	
b. No	☐	If you checked No at left, skip to Q. 19

18. Please describe your current or future initiatives on this matter.

19. Please provide the following information on the sources of your institution's data on remittance **inflows** by answering the applicable questions in Table 7 below.

Table 7

	i. Source of data on remittance inflows (Yes/No)? If yes, since what year?	ii. If applicable: Do national regulations require this source to submit remittances inflows data to the relevant authority? (Y/N)	iii. If applicable: How often must this source submit remittances inflows data to the relevant authority? (for example monthly, quarterly, annually, etc.)	iv. If applicable: How does this source provide remittances inflows data to the relevant authority: by post, fax, email, other (please specify)?
a) Firms specialized in money transfers (Western Union, Money Gram, etc.)				
b) Private commercial banks				
c) State-owned banks				
d) Exchange bureaus				
e) Microfinance institutions				
f) Savings and loan institutions				
g) Credit unions and savings cooperatives				
h) Other financial institutions that receive and/or send remittances: please specify				
i) Post offices				
j) Mobile phone/telecoms service providers				
k) Other non-financial institutions that deliver remittances: please specify				
l) Settlement and clearance agencies				
m) Information reported by migrants entering the country (at airports and other points of entry)				
n) Surveys of households				
o) Surveys on spending by tourists/visitors to your country (which include data collection on visiting nationals of your country now residing overseas and carrying remittances by hand)				
p) Other; please specify:				

20. What types of transactions do you record as migrant remittance **inflows**? Please check all that apply.

a. Bank draft payments	☐
b. Checks issued by banks in foreign jurisdictions	☐
c. International money orders sent by post	☐
d. International money orders sent electronically	☐
e. Electronic fund transfers through correspondent banks	☐
f. Electronic fund transfers from remitter's bank directly to debit or prepaid card held by remittance recipient	☐
g. Use of pre-paid and debit cards for remittances at retail stores in your country	☐
h. Electronic transfer of remittances to the mobile phone of a remittance recipient in your country	☐
i. Withdrawals at automated teller machines (ATMs) in your country by remittance recipients using cards issued by foreign financial institutions	☐
j. Remittance inflows received by firms specialized in cross-border money transfer operations (Money Gram, Western Union)	☐
k. Money reported at airports/other points of entry to your country by migrants returning for visits	☐
l. Purchase of a home or other real estate in your country by migrants from your country residing overseas for the use of beneficiaries in your country	☐
m. Other: please specify	☐

21. Which methods are used by your institution in collecting data and other information on migrant remittance **inflows**? Please check all that apply.

a. Data collected from the banking system	☐
b. Reporting of data on these flows by nonbanks that provide remittance services	☐
c. Estimates of these flows using surveys	☐
d. Calculating migrants "propensity to remit" estimates	☐

22. Does the data you collect allow you to identify the **source country** of remittance **inflows**?

a. Yes	☐		b. No	☐

23. Does the data you collect allow you to identify the **number** of remittance **inflow** transactions?

a. Yes	☐		b. No	☐

24. Is there some means through which the central bank and/or some other relevant national institution estimates remittance **inflows** through **informal** channels?

a. Yes	☐	
b. No	☐	If you checked No at left, skip to Q. 27

25. How have remittance **inflows** through **informal** channels been estimated? Please check all that apply.

a. Data collection at airports and other points of entry on cash carried across your borders to remittance recipients residing in your country by visiting nationals now residing overseas.	☐
b. Data collection on cash carried across your borders by courier transport companies that is delivered to remittance recipients residing in your country	☐
c. Other; please specify	☐

26. Have remittance **inflows** through **informal** channels been estimated on:

a. A one-off basis	☐	If you checked at left, when?
b. An ad hoc basis	☐	If you checked at left, when?
c. Periodic basis	☐	If you checked at left, how frequently?
d. Other	☐	If you checked at left, please specify:

27. Aside from your institution, are there other institutions and/or government agencies in your country collecting and compiling national data and other information from multiple sources on remittance **inflows**?

a. Yes	☐	
b. No	☐	If you checked No at left, skip to Section III, question 32

28. Please indicate which institutions compile these data in your country.

a. National statistics office/agency	☐
b. Ministry of Finance	☐
c. Ministry of Tourism	☐
d. Labor Ministry	☐
e. Other; please specify:	☐

29. How does the collection of data on cross-border remittance **inflows** by the institution(s) indicated above differ from that compiled by your institution?

30. Does your institution and/or the institution(s) indicated in Q. 28 have an arrangement in place to exchange data and information on remittance **inflows** on a regular basis?

a. Yes	☐	
b. No	☐	If you checked No at left, skip to Section III, question 32

31. Please indicate below how often these data are exchanged?

a. Monthly	☐
b. Quarterly	☐
c. Annually	☐
d. Other; please specify:	☐

III. National Regulatory Environment for Migrant Remittance Flows

A. Registration, supervisory and other regulatory requirements

32. Is your institution(s) responsible for regulating cross-border migrant remittance flows in your country?

a. Yes	☐	
b. No, it is another institution(s): please specify	☐	If you checked No at left, skip to Section IV, question 82

33. According to your laws, which of the institutions below in Table 8 can receive and/or send cross-border remittance flows?

Table 8

	i. Receives remittance inflows from foreign sources intended for beneficiaries in your country? Indicate Yes/No	ii. If yes to Question ii, what is the national supervisory authority for this institution's remittance service activities?	iii. Sends remittance outflows from migrants in your country to beneficiaries abroad? Indicate Yes/No	iv. If yes to Question iii, what is the national supervisory authority for this institution's remittance service activities?
a) Firms specialized in money transfers (Western Union, Money Gram, etc.)				
b) Private commercial banks				
c) State-owned banks				
d) Exchange bureaus				
e) Microfinance institutions				
f) Savings and loan institutions				
g) Credit unions and savings cooperatives				
h) Other financial institutions that deliver remittances; please specify:				
i) Post offices				
j) Mobile phone/telecoms service providers				
k) Other non-financial institutions that deliver remittances: specify:				

34. For each of the types of institutions listed in Table 9 that can receive and/or send cross-border remittance flows (remittance service providers), please answer the following questions on regulatory requirements related to the provision of remittance services.

Table 9

	i. Are these institutions legally obligated to have a formal partnership with a bank in order to receive remittance inflows? Indicate Yes//No. (Please answer for all applicable.)	ii. Are these institutions legally obligated to have a formal partnership with a bank in order to send remittance outflows? Indicate Yes/No. (Please answer for all applicable.)	iii. If applicable, what are the obligations and/or restrictions to which these institutions are subject under these partnerships with banks?
a) Firms specialized in money transfers (Western Union, Money Gram, etc.)			
b) Exchange bureaus			
c) Microfinance institutions			
d) Savings and loan institutions			
e) Credit unions and savings cooperatives			
f) Other financial institutions that receive and/or send remittances: please specify			
g) Post offices			
h) Mobile phone/telecoms service providers			
i) Other non-financial institutions that deliver remittances: please specify			

B. Reporting requirements for remittance inflows

35. Does your institution's statute or charter state explicitly that monitoring of remittance **inflows** is among your institution's functions?

a. Yes	☐	
b. No	☐	

36. Are there reporting requirements with which institutions that receive and deliver cross-border remittance **inflows** must comply?

a. Yes	☐	
b. No	☐	If you checked No at left, skip to Section III.C, Question 45

37. If yes, to Q. 36, please provide the following requested information in Table 10 on reporting requirements for each type of institution in your country that receives and delivers remittance **inflows**.

Table 10

	i. Please mark with an "X" below if the institution is required to report remittance inflows to your institution.	ii. Please list if there is another institution to which remittance inflows must be reported.
a) Firms specialized in money transfers (Western Union, Money Gram, etc.)	☐	
b) Private commercial banks	☐	
c) State-owned banks	☐	
d) Exchange bureaus	☐	
e) Microfinance institutions	☐	
f) Savings and loan institutions	☐	
g) Credit unions and savings cooperatives	☐	
h) Other financial institutions that deliver remittances: please specify	☐	
i) Post offices	☐	
j) Mobile phone/telecoms service providers	☐	
k) Other non-financial institutions that deliver remittances: please specify	☐	

38. Please indicate below the specific types of information that must be reported by each type of institution that is required to report remittance **inflows** to your institution.

a. Remittance inflows transaction amounts	☐
b. Remittances "sending country" (that is, the country in which the remittances sender is based)	☐
c. Specific instrument used to transmit remittances to recipients in your country	☐
d. The mandatory information to be reported depends on (varies by) the type of remittances service provider	☐
e. Other: please specify	☐

39. If you checked d. in Q. 38 above, would you please specify how the type(s) of mandatory information on remittance **inflows** reported to your institution varies by type of remittances services provider.

40. Please indicate whether remittance service providers in your country are:

a. Required to report each separate cross-border remittance **inflows** transaction	☐
b. Able to report multiple cross-border remittance **inflows** transactions periodically	☐
c. The answer depends on (varies by) the type of remittances service provider	☐

41. If you checked c. in Q. 40 above, would you please list the type(s) of remittance service providers in your country that are required to report each separate cross-border remittance **inflows** transaction

42. If you checked b. or c. in Q. 40, would you please indicate how often remittance service providers in your country are required to make reports of multiple cross-border remittance **inflows** transactions:

a. Daily	☐
b. Weekly	☐
c. Monthly	☐
d. Quarterly	☐
e. Other: please specify	☐

43. Do the reporting requirements for cross-border remittance **inflows** transactions apply only at specific remittance thresholds (that is, above a specified remittance amount)?

a. Yes	☐		b. No	☐

44. If yes to Q. 43, what is this threshold?

C. Reporting requirements for remittance outflows

45. Does your institution's statute or charter state explicitly that monitoring of remittance **outflows** is among your institution's functions?

a. Yes	☐	
b. No	☐	

46. Are there reporting requirements with which institutions that send cross-border remittance **outflows** must comply?

a. Yes	☐	
b. No	☐	If you checked No at left, skip to Question 55

47. If yes, to Q. 46, please provide the following requested information in Table 11 on reporting requirements for each type of institution in your country that accepts remittances from senders in your country and sends these cross-border remittance **outflows** to beneficiaries abroad.

Table 11

	i. Please mark with an "X" if the institution is required to report remittance outflows to your institution	ii. Please list if there is another institution(s)/ government agency(ies) to which remittance outflows must be reported
a. Firms specialized in money transfers (Western Union, Money Gram, etc.)	☐	
b. Private commercial banks	☐	
c. State-owned banks	☐	
d. Exchange bureaus	☐	
e. Microfinance institutions	☐	
f. Savings and loan institutions	☐	
g. Credit unions and savings cooperatives	☐	
h. Other financial institutions that deliver remittances: please specify	☐	
i. Post offices	☐	
j. Mobile phone/telecoms service providers	☐	
k. Other non-financial institutions that deliver remittances: please specify	☐	

48. Please indicate below the specific types of information that must be reported by each type of institution that is required to report remittance **outflows** to your institution.

a. Remittance **outflows** transaction amounts	☐
b. Remittances "**destination country**" (that is, the country in which the remittances recipient is based)	☐
c. Specific instrument used to transmit remittances by senders in your country	☐
d. The mandatory information to be reported depends on (varies by) the type of remittances service provider	☐
e. Other: please specify	☐

49. If you checked d. in Q. 48 above, would you please specify how the type(s) of mandatory information on remittance **outflows** reported to your institution varies by type of remittances services provider.

50. Please indicate whether remittance service providers in your country are:

a. Required to report each separate cross-border remittance **outflows** transaction	☐
b. Are able to report multiple cross-border remittance **outflows** transactions periodically	☐
c. Options a. and b.: Answer depends on/varies by type of remittances service provider	☐

51. If you checked c. in Q. 50 above, would you please list the type(s) of remittance service providers in your country that are required to report each separate cross-border remittance **outflows** transaction.

52. If you checked b. or c. in Q. 50, would you please indicate how often remittance service providers in your country are required to make periodic reports to the relevant national authorities of multiple cross-border remittance **outflows** transactions:

a. Daily	☐
b. Weekly	☐
c. Monthly	☐
d. Quarterly	☐
e. Other: please specify	☐

53. Do the reporting requirements for cross-border remittance **outflows** transactions apply only at specific remittance thresholds (that is, above a specified remittance amount)?

a. Yes	☐		b. No	☐

54. If yes to Q. 53, what is(are) the threshold amount(s)?

55. Have there been any recent or planned regulatory initiatives to seek to harmonize the reporting requirements with which cross-border remittance service providers in your country must comply?

a. Yes	☐		b. No	☐

56. If yes to Q. 55, would you please briefly describe those initiatives, the type(s) of remittance service providers to which these would apply, and the timing of these initiatives (that is, specify dates of implementation if possible)?

D. National policies for anti-money laundering and combating the financing of terrorism

57. Is your institution involved in developing and/or implementing national policies for anti-money laundering and combating the financing of terrorism?

a. Yes	☐	
b. No	☐	If you checked No at left, skip to Section III.E, Question 65

58. What are the specific sanctions that are imposed in your country with regards to violations of regulations to prevent money laundering and to combat the financing of terrorism? Please check all that apply.

a. Fines for institutions and/or individuals who facilitate money laundering or the funding of terrorism	☐
b. Court-ordered freezing of funds involved in the particular transaction(s)	☐
c. Imprisonment	☐
d. Other: please specify	☐

59. Which entity(ies) in your countries enforce(s) these sanctions?

a. Central bank	☐
b. Ministry of finance	☐
c. A separate national (or regional) authority set up and specifically charged with preventing money laundering	☐
d. Other: please specify	☐

60. Is there a wing for anti-money laundering/combating the financing of terrorism within your country's general law enforcement authorities, which cooperates with your or other national authorities on compliance/enforcement matters?

a. Yes	☐	b. No	☐

61. Are there plans to enhance national regulations and mechanisms to prevent money laundering and to combat the financing of terrorism in your country?

a. Yes	☐	b. No	☐

62. If yes, to Q. 61, please describe these plans and envisaged date(s) for implementation.

63. Please provide the following further information in Table 12 on reporting requirements and associated documentation for each type of institution in your country that receives and/or sends cross-border remittance flows.

Table 12

	i. Are these remittance service providers obliged to file currency transaction reports? If yes, to which national authority?	ii. If yes to Q.i., is there an amount threshold for filing currency transaction reports? Please specify threshold	iii. Are there limits imposed on daily transaction amounts per customer? Please specify these limits	iv. Are these remittance service providers obliged to file suspicious activity reports? If yes, to which national authority?	v. If yes to Q.iv., is there an amount threshold for filing suspicious transaction reports? Please specify threshold
a. Firms specialized in money transfers (Western Union, Money Gram, etc.)					
b. Private commercial banks					
c. State-owned banks					
d. Exchange bureaus					
e. Microfinance institutions					
f. Savings and loan institutions					
g. Credit unions and savings cooperatives					
h. Other financial institutions that deliver remittances: please specify					
i. Post offices					
j. Mobile phone/telecoms service providers					
k. Other non-financial institutions that deliver remittances: please specify					

64. What additional regulations and mechanisms are currently in place to prevent money laundering and to combat the financing of terrorism in your country?

E. Foreign exchange regulations and related costs

65. Is your institution involved in developing and/or implementing national foreign exchange regulations?

a. Yes	☐	
b. No	☐	If you checked No at left, skip to Section IV, Question 82

66. Is it compulsory for recipients of remittance **inflows** in your country to convert the remittances into **local currency**?

| a. Yes ☐ | b. No ☐ |

67. Is there a ceiling that applies specifically for remittance **inflows** that are not converted into **local currency**?

| a. Yes ☐ | b. No ☐ |

68. If yes to Q. 67, what is this ceiling and the corresponding time period to which it applies?

69. Can people residing in your country send cross-border remittances (remittance **outflows**) denominated in **foreign currency** to recipients residing abroad?

| a. Yes ☐ | b. No ☐ |

70. Is there a remittance ceiling that applies specifically for remittance **outflows** that are denominated in **foreign currency**?

| a. Yes ☐ | b. No ☐ |

71. If yes to Q. 70, what is this ceiling and the corresponding time period to which it applies?

72. Can people residing in your country send cross-border remittances (remittance **outflows**) denominated in **local currency** to recipients residing abroad?

| a. Yes ☐ | b. No ☐ |

73. Is there a remittance ceiling that applies specifically for remittance **outflows** that are denominated in **local currency**?

| a. Yes ☐ | b. No ☐ |

74. If yes to Q. 73, what is this ceiling and the corresponding time period to which it applies?

75. Does the central bank have any legal powers to issue regulations to limit the costs related to the exchange rate to be used for remittance transactions?

| a. Yes ☐ | b. No ☐ |

76. If yes to Q. 75, has the central bank used these legal powers in order to lower currency conversion costs for remittances in the past five years?

| a. Yes ☐ | b. No ☐ |

77. If yes to Q. 75, how and when?

78. Does your country allow the general public to have deposit accounts in foreign currencies?

a. Yes	☐		b. No	☐

79. How do foreign exchange regulations related to cross-border remittance flows vary for different remittance service providers in your country? Please answer below for all applicable remittance service providers in your country.

Table 13

	i. Is this institution prohibited from handling foreign exchange transactions independently? Y/N	ii. Does the relevant regulatory authority place limits on this institution's amount of foreign exchange holdings or remittance inflows? Y/N	iii. Does the relevant regulatory authority place limits on this institution's remittance outflows? Y/N	iv. If yes to Q. ii and/or iii , what are these limits?
a. Firms specialized in money transfers (Western Union, Money Gram, etc.)				
b. Private commercial banks				
c. State-owned banks				
d. Exchange bureaus				
e. Microfinance institutions				
f. Savings and loan institutions				
g. Credit unions and savings cooperatives				
h. Other financial institutions that deliver remittances: please specify				
i. Post offices				
j. Mobile phone/telecoms service providers				
k. Other non-financial institutions that deliver remittances: please specify				

80. Does the central bank have any legal powers to issue regulations to limit the costs related to the transfer and/or sending of cross-border remittances?

a. Yes	☐		b. No	☐

81. If yes to Q. 80, has the central bank used these legal powers in order to lower these costs in the past five years?

a. Yes	☐	If you checked yes at left, how and when?
b. No	☐	

IV. Financial Infrastructure Supporting Cross-border Remittance Flows

> *This set of questions is intended to examine the extent to which current national financial infrastructure supports and facilitates cross-border remittance flows transmitted by all types of remittance service providers. This section is intended to take stock of recent and upcoming changes in national policy that would expand the access of various RSPs to financial infrastructure/systems and/or expand the outreach of remittance services to remote locations.*

82. Please answer the questions in Table 14 about access to clearing and settlement systems by the remittance service providers in your country.

Table 14

	i. Has access to the central bank's clearing and settlement systems? Yes/No	ii. If applicable, are there plans to expand these institutions' access to these systems? Yes/No	iii. If applicable, what clearing and settlement systems do these institutions use?
a. Firms specialized in money transfers (Western Union, Money Gram, etc.)			
b. Private commercial banks			
c. State-owned banks			
d. Exchange bureaus			
e. Microfinance institutions			
f. Savings and loan institutions			
g. Credit unions and savings cooperatives			
h. Other financial institutions that deliver remittances: please specify			
i. Post offices			
j. Mobile phone/telecommunications service providers			
k. Other nonfinancial institutions that deliver remittances: please specify			

83. Are there any recent moves or plans to implement a common payment platform in your country and/or region, which would facilitate remittance transfers?

a. Yes	☐	b. No	☐

84. If yes to Q. 83, please describe these initiatives indicating implementation dates.

85. If yes to Q. 83, are/will all ATM and point of sale devices be linked/compatible with the common payment platform?

a. Yes	☐	b. No	☐

86. Have there been any initiatives by financial authorities to expand the outreach of remittances services to rural areas/remote locations in your country?

a. Yes	☐		b. No	☐

87. If yes to Q. 86, please briefly describe these initiatives, indicating implementation dates.

V. Best Practices, Public Policy Issues, Agreements for Data, and Technology Sharing

By taking a cross-country inventory of national authorities' views on best practices and important public policy issues, as well as the extent to which countries have negotiated data and/or technology sharing agreements to improve information and/or efficiency of systems, this set of questions seeks to gauge emerging priority policy issues and practices for the region and the extent to which countries make use of and benefit from collaborative agreements in this area.

88. From your perspective, are any of the following areas in need of improved policy coordination within your country? Please check all that apply.

a. Eliminating inconsistencies within national policy vis-à-vis remittance flows. Please specify	☐
b. Better management of the tension between improving financial access and avoiding financial crime.	☐
c. Other: please specify	☐

89. From your perspective, what are the areas that require more attention in order to make the transfer and delivery of remittances more efficient and secure? Please select all applicable areas.

a. Better statistics on remittances	☐
b. Better statistics and studies on migrants	☐
c. Increased competition among remittance service providers	☐
d. Delivery of remittances to remote areas	☐
e. New technologies and products for the provision of remittance services	☐
f. Financial integrity issues	☐
g. Other: please specify	☐

90. In your opinion, are there any practices that should be prohibited in order to make the transfer and delivery of cross-border remittances more secure?

91. Does your country restrict the sending of remittances to certain countries?

a. Yes	☐		b. No	☐

92. If applicable to which countries is the sending of remittances restricted?

93. Are there any formal or informal arrangements of which you are aware for data-sharing on cross-border remittance flows between institutions in your country and counterpart authorities in other countries?

a. Yes	☐	
b. No	☐	If you checked no at left, please skip to Q. 97

94. Would you please specify with which countries' national authorities your institution shares/exchanges data on cross-border remittance flows?

a)
b)
c)
d)

95. Would you please specify the type(s) of remittance data shared?

96. Please indicate below how often these data are exchanged.

a. Monthly	☐
b. Quarterly	☐
c. Annually	☐
d. Other; Please specify	☐

97. Are there any arrangements of which you are aware between national institutions and their counterparts in other countries that aim to improve the efficiency of cross-border remittance transmissions?

a. Yes	☐	
b. No	☐	If you checked no at left, please skip to Q. 100

98. Would you please specify with which countries' institutions these arrangements have been made?

a)
b)
c)
d)
e)

99. Would you please specify how these arrangements aim to improve the efficiency of cross-border remittance transmissions?

100. Is there any office in your country responsible for handling and resolving complaints of the clients of remittance service providers (that is, remittance recipients and/or senders) on issues related to the provision of cross-border remittance services?

a) Yes	☐		b) No	☐

101. If yes to Q. 100, what is the office?

102. If there is no such entity, how are those issues normally resolved?

103. What may be, in your opinion, inhibiting migrants residing abroad from using formal channels to transfer cross-border remittance to recipients in your country? Please check all that apply.

a. Sender's lack of valid identification in host country	☐
b. No bank branch near residence of beneficiary	☐
c. Remittances recipient's lack of access to bank accounts	☐
d. Mistrust of formal financial institutions	☐
e. Mistrust or lack of information about electronic transfers	☐
f. National payments systems' lack of capacity to transfer remittances quickly	☐
g. Foreign exchange controls	☐
h. High costs of services	☐
i. Sending country's tax policies on remittance outflows	☐
j. Your country's tax policies on remittance inflows	☐
k. Other: please specify	☐

104. In your opinion, what needs to be done in your own country to encourage immigrants to transfer remittances to recipients abroad through formal channels? Please check all that apply.

a. Lift foreign exchange restrictions	☐
b. Allow remittance outflows to be denominated in any international currency and not just in local currency.	☐
c. Improve access to banking services of senders living in remote areas.	☐
d. Change senders'/public perception of formal financial institutions.	☐
e. Improve public awareness of innovative technologies available for remittance transfer.	☐
f. Improve postal service infrastructure to be able to deliver remittances to more locations	☐
g. Eliminate exclusivity contracts between money transfer operators and other institutions delivering remittances.	☐
h. Revise tax policies affecting remittances	☐
i. Other: please specify	☐

105. What incentives do you grant migrants living abroad to transfer their money back to your country?

a. Attractive investment options	☐
b. Tax breaks	☐
c. Matching funds for remittance-backed projects	☐
d. Other: Please specify	☐

106. Are there any plans to foster the use of formal mechanisms to transfer remittances, instead of informal channels?

a) Yes	☐		b) No	☐

107. If yes to Q. 106, please describe these initiatives:

108. Do you have any plans to make use of the amount of funds your country receives in remittances each year to obtain additional financing in the local or international markets (for example securitizing future flows of remittances)? If so, please describe these initiatives.

Thank you for completing the survey and participating in our study.

Appendix 2. Survey Questionnaire: Focus On Remittance Outflows

Introduction and Outline

Thank you for taking the time to complete our survey on the national regulatory environment for migrants' cross-border remittance flows, monitoring practices, and migrant cross-border remittances data. This survey is part of a larger cross-country data and information collection exercise intended to fill the knowledge gap on the impact of migrant remittances on development. The findings from this survey, which is being sent to central banks and other relevant national authorities worldwide, are intended to help inform future efforts to strengthen the capacity of national policy makers and institutions to analyze relevant trends and determinants of these capital flows in order to enhance their development impact.

The survey questionnaire that follows is structured in five main sections, following the outline below. Please complete all of the questions that are relevant to your country's particular situation as a recipient and/or source of remittance flows.

Section I. Recent data collected on remittance outflows

Section II. Data collection practices: Remittance outflows

Section III. National regulatory environment for migrant remittance flows

Section IV. Financial infrastructure supporting cross-border remittance flows

Section V. Best Practices, Public Policy Issues, Bilateral Agreements for Data and Technology Sharing

---

Please return the completed questionnaire to the World Bank Group, to the attention of Mr. Dilip Ratha, Manager, Migration & Remittances Team, World Bank Group, 1818 H Street, NW, Washington, DC 20433, USA, Fax +1-202-522-3564, Email: Dratha@worldbank.org

---

Name of person(s) responding to this questionnaire:

Position and Department/Division:

Institution and location (city, country):

Phone number:

Email address:

Date questionnaire completed (dd/mm/yyyy):

Are you completing this questionnaire on the behalf of another colleague(s)? If yes, please provide the name(s), position(s), department(s) and contact details for that colleague(s) below.

I. Recent Data Collected on Remittance Outflows

> *By compiling available national data on migrant remittance flows, responses to this set of questions will improve the understanding of the magnitude and characteristics of remittance flows, with a view to generating informed policy recommendations that would maximize their positive development impact.*

1. Does your institution collect data on cross-border remittance **outflows**?

a. Yes	☐	
b. No, it is another institution(s): please specify:	☐	If you checked No at left, skip to Section III, Question 32

2. According to your estimates, what is the annual volume of cross-border remittance **outflows** from your country since 2005?

Table 1

	i. Workers' remittance outflows (US$)	ii. Compensation of employees (US$)	iii. Migrants' transfers (outflows by migrants employed in your economy) (US$)	iv. Total (US$)	v. Informal remittance outflows (US$)
a) 2007 (forecast)					
b) 2006					
c) 2005					
Please also provide these data for earlier years if available:					
d) 2004					
e) 2003					
f) 2002					

3. According to your most recently available estimates for annual remittance **outflows**, please list the top destination countries for cross-border remittance flows sent from your country by ranking from 1 to 10 in Table 2 below, with a rank of 1 going to the top destination country for remittance **outflows**. If data are available, please provide estimates of the amount of these annual remittance **outflows** by destination country in the table's second column.

Table 2

i. Top destination countries (List as many as possible)	ii. Estimated amount of annual remittance outflows for most recently available year (US$) Specify year:
1)	
2)	
3)	
4)	
5)	
6)	
7)	
8)	
9)	
10)	

4. For the top 10 destination countries that you listed in Question 3, please briefly note below what you believe to be the main factor(s) driving remittance **outflows** to this country.

Table 3

i. Top destination countries (List as many as possible)	ii. What are the main factor(s) driving remittance outflows to this country?
1)	
2)	
3)	
4)	
5)	
6)	
7)	
8)	
9)	
10)	

5. Would you please provide as much of the following data as are available on remittance **outflows** for each applicable transfer instrument for the most recent two-year period in Table 4? Please be sure to specify the actual year (indicating whether it is calendar or fiscal year). Please indicate the currency of denomination if other than U.S. dollars.

Table 4

Instrument to transfer cross-border remittance outflows	Year 1 (specify year:)		Year 2 (specify year:)	
	i. Number of transactions	ii. Volume of transactions (US$)	iii. Number of transactions	iv. Volume of transactions (US$)
a) Bank drafts				
b) Checks issued by banks				
c) International money orders sent by post				
d) International money orders sent electronically				
e) Electronic wire via money transfer operators (for example, Money Gram, Western Union)s				
f) Electronic fund transfers through correspondent banks				
g) Debit cards				
h) Pre-paid cards				
i) Money reported at airports/borders carried by relatives traveling to home country				
j) Money transfer by mobile phone				
k) Other, please specify				
l) Total				

6. Are there particular periods of the year when remittance **outflows** tend to be much larger or much smaller?

a. Yes	☐		b. No	☐

7. Does your country employ migrants under guest-worker programs?

a. Yes	☐	☐	If you checked Yes at left, please go to Q. 8
b. No	☐	☐	If you checked No at left, go to Q. 9

8. Please indicate below with which country(ies) and sector(s) of the economy these guest worker programs are in effect?

i. Country	ii. Sector
a)	
b)	
c)	
d)	

9. If applicable: During which seasons/periods of the year are remittance **outflows** likely to be larger?

10. If applicable: During which seasons/periods of the year are remittance **outflows** likely to be smaller?

11. Please complete Table 5 for each type of institution listed below that transmits remittance **outflows** from senders in your country to recipients abroad at present. Please provide estimates, if necessary.

Table 5

	i. Number of institutions	ii. Total number of branches	iii. Number of branches in rural areas
a) Firms specialized in money transfers (Western Union, Money Gram, etc.)			
b) Private commercial banks			
c) State-owned banks			
d) Exchange bureaus			
e) Microfinance institutions			
f) Savings and loan institutions			
g) Credit unions and savings cooperatives			
h) Other financial institutions that transmit remittances: please specify			
i) Post offices			
j) Mobile phone/telecoms service providers			
k) Other non-financial institutions that transmit remittances: please specify			

II. Data Collection Practices: Remittance Outflows

Effective national data collection and other systems and procedures for monitoring migrant remittance flows help enable national policy makers to devise appropriate policies that would promote the beneficial development effects of remittances. This set of questions aims to take an inventory of national data collection practices to assess national capacity in this area on a cross-country basis.

12. Which division(s) within your institution currently is(are) responsible for collecting data on remittance **outflows**?

13. How long ago did your institution first begin collecting data and information on remittance **outflows**?

a. Over the past year	☐
b. 2-5 years ago	☐
c. 6-10 years ago	☐
d. 11-20 years ago	☐
e. More than 20 years ago	☐
f. Other: please specify	☐

14. How often does your institution collect data and information on remittance **outflows**?

a. Monthly	☐
b. Quarterly	☐
c. Semi-annually	☐
d. Annually	☐
e. Occasionally	☐
f. Other: please specify	☐

15. Other than changes in data collection frequency, have your data collection practices for remittance **outflows** changed in other ways over the past five years?

a. Yes	☐	
b. No	☐	If you checked No at left, skip to Q. 17

16. Please indicate the ways in which these practices have changed. Check all that apply.

a. In terms of types of data compiled	☐	Please specify how:	
b. In terms of changes in sources of data	☐	Please specify how:	
c. Other	☐	Please specify:	

17. Do you have any plans to change the coverage of your data on remittances **outflows** and/or the methodology used to measure remittances?

a. Yes	☐	
b. No	☐	If you checked No at left, skip to Q. 19

18. Please describe your current or future initiatives on this matter.

19. Please provide the following information on the sources of your institution's data on remittance **outflows** by answering the applicable questions in Table 7 below.

Table 7

	i. Source of data on remittance outflows (Yes/No)? If yes, since what year?	ii. If applicable: Do national regulations require this source to submit remittances outflows data to the relevant authority? (Y/N)	iii. If applicable: How often must this source submit remittances outflows data to the relevant authority? (e.g. monthly, quarterly, annually, etc.)	iv. If applicable: How does this source provide remittances outflows data to the relevant authority: by post, fax, email, other (please specify)?
a) Firms specialized in money transfers (Western Union, Money Gram, etc.)				
b) Private commercial banks				
c) State-owned banks				
d) Exchange bureaus				
e) Microfinance institutions				
f) Savings and loan institutions				
g) Credit unions and savings cooperatives				
h) Other financial institutions that transmit remittances: please specify				
i) Post offices				
j) Mobile phone/telecoms service providers				
k) Other non-financial institutions that transmit remittances: please specify				
l) Settlement and clearance agencies				
m) Information reported by migrants exiting the country (at airports and other points of exit)				
n) Surveys of households				
o) Other; please specify:				

20. What types of transactions do you record as migrant remittance **outflows**? Please check all that apply.

a. Bank draft payments	☐
b. Checks issued by banks	☐
c. International money orders sent by post	☐
d. International money orders sent electronically	☐
e. Electronic fund transfers through correspondent banks	☐
f. Electronic fund transfers from remitter's bank in your country directly to debit or prepaid card held by remittance recipient	☐
g. Electronic transfer of remittances via mobile phone by a remitter in your country to a recipient located abroad	☐
h. Remittance outflows sent by firms specialized in cross-border money transfer operations (Money Gram, Western Union)	☐
i. Money reported at airports/other points of exit from your country, carried by immigrants on returning to their home countries for visits	☐
j. Purchase of a home or other real estate abroad by immigrants residing in your country for the use of beneficiaries abroad	☐
k. Other: please specify	☐

21. Which methods are used by your institution in collecting data and other information on migrant remittance **outflows**? Please check all that apply.

a. Data collected from the banking system	☐
b. Reporting of data on these flows by nonbanks that provide remittance services	☐
c. Estimates of these flows using surveys	☐
d. Calculating migrants "propensity to remit" estimates	☐

22. Does the data you collect allow you to identify the **destination country** for remittance **outflows**?

a. Yes	☐		b. No	☐

23. Does the data you collect allow you to identify the **number** of remittance **outflow** transactions?

a. Yes	☐		b. No	☐

24. Is there some means through which the central bank and/or some other relevant national institution estimates remittance **outflows** through **informal** channels?

a. Yes	☐	
b. No	☐	If you checked No at left, skip to Q. 27

25. How have remittance **outflows** through **informal** channels been estimated? Please check all that apply.

a. Data collection at airports and other points of exit on cash carried across your borders to remittance recipients residing abroad by immigrants on returning to their home countries for visits.	☐
b. Data collection on cash carried across your borders by courier transport companies that is delivered to remittance recipients residing abroad	☐
c. Other; please specify	☐

26. Have remittance **outflows** through **informal** channels been estimated on:

a. A one-off basis	☐	If you checked at left, when?
b. An ad hoc basis	☐	If you checked at left, when?
c. Periodic basis	☐	If you checked at left, how frequently?
d. Other	☐	If you checked at left, please specify:

27. Aside from your institution, are there other institutions and/or government agencies in your country collecting and compiling national data and other information from multiple sources on remittance **outflows** from your country?

a. Yes	☐	
b. No	☐	If you checked No at left, skip to Section III, question 32

28. Please indicate which institutions in your country compile data on remittance **outflows**.

a. National statistics office/agency	☐
b. Ministry of Finance	☐
c. Ministry of Tourism	☐
d. Labor Ministry	☐
e. Other; please specify:	☐

29. How does the collection of data on cross-border remittance **outflows** by the institution(s) indicated above differ from that compiled by your institution?

30. Does your institution and/or the institution(s) indicated in Q. 28 have an arrangement in place to exchange data and information on remittance **outflows** on a regular basis?

a. Yes	☐	
b. No	☐	If you checked No at left, skip to Section III, question 32

31. Please indicate below how often these data are exchanged?

a. Monthly	☐
b. Quarterly	☐
c. Annually	☐
d. Other; please specify:	☐

III. National Regulatory Environment for Migrant Remittance Flows

A. Registration, supervisory and other regulatory requirements

32. Is your institution(s) responsible for regulating cross-border migrant remittance flows in your country?

a. Yes	☐	
b. No, it is another institution(s): please specify	☐	If you checked No at left, skip to Section IV, question 82

33. According to your laws, which of the institutions below in Table 8 can receive and/or send cross-border remittance flows?

Table 8

	i. Receives remittance inflows from foreign sources intended for beneficiaries in your country? Indicate Yes/No	ii. If yes to Question i, what is the national supervisory authority for this institution's remittance service activities?	iii. Sends remittance outflows from migrants in your country to beneficiaries abroad? Indicate Yes/No	iv. If yes to Question iii, what is the national supervisory authority for this institution's remittance service activities?
a) Firms specialized in money transfers (Western Union, Money Gram, etc.)				
b) Private commercial banks				
c) State-owned banks				
d) Exchange bureaus				
e) Microfinance institutions				
f) Savings and loan institutions				
g) Credit unions and savings cooperatives				
h) Other financial institutions that deliver remittances; please specify:				
i) Post offices				
j) Mobile phone/telecoms service providers				
k) Other non-financial institutions that deliver remittances: specify:				

34. For each of the types of institutions listed in Table 9 that can receive and/or send cross-border remittance flows (remittance service providers), please answer the following questions on regulatory requirements related to the provision of remittance services.

Table 9

	i. Are these institutions legally obligated to have a formal partnership with a bank in order to receive remittance inflows? Indicate Yes//No. (Please answer for all applicable.)	ii. Are these institutions legally obligated to have a formal partnership with a bank in order to send remittance outflows? Indicate Yes/No. (Please answer for all applicable.)	iii. If applicable, what are the obligations and/or restrictions to which these institutions are subject under these partnerships with banks?
a) Firms specialized in money transfers (Western Union, Money Gram, etc.)			
b) Exchange bureaus			
c) Microfinance institutions			
d) Savings and loan institutions			
e) Credit unions and savings cooperatives			
f) Other financial institutions that receive and/or send remittances: please specify			
g) Post offices			
h) Mobile phone/telecoms service providers			
i) Other non-financial institutions that deliver remittances: please specify			

B. Reporting requirements for remittance inflows

35. Does your institution's statute or charter state explicitly that monitoring of remittance **inflows** is among your institution's functions?

a. Yes	☐	
b. No	☐	

36. Are there reporting requirements with which institutions that receive and deliver cross-border remittance **inflows** must comply?

a. Yes	☐	
b. No	☐	If you checked No at left, skip to Section III.C, Question 45

37. If yes, to Q. 36, please provide the following requested information in Table 10 on reporting requirements for each type of institution in your country that receives and delivers remittance **inflows**.

Table 10

	i. Please mark with an "X" below if the institution is required to report remittance inflows to your institution.	ii. Please list if there is another institution to which remittance inflows must be reported.
a) Firms specialized in money transfers (Western Union, Money Gram, etc.)	☐	
b) Private commercial banks	☐	
c) State-owned banks	☐	
d) Exchange bureaus	☐	
e) Microfinance institutions	☐	
f) Savings and loan institutions	☐	
g) Credit unions and savings cooperatives	☐	
h) Other financial institutions that deliver remittances: please specify	☐	
i) Post offices	☐	
j) Mobile phone/telecoms service providers	☐	
k) Other non-financial institutions that deliver remittances: please specify	☐	

38. Please indicate below the specific types of information that must be reported by each type of institution that is required to report remittance **inflows** to your institution.

a. Remittance inflows transaction amounts	☐
b. Remittances "sending country" (that is, the country in which the remittances sender is based)	☐
c. Specific instrument used to transmit remittances to recipients in your country	☐
d. The mandatory information to be reported depends on (varies by) the type of remittances service provider	☐
e. Other: please specify	☐

39. If you checked d. in Q. 38 above, would you please specify how the type(s) of mandatory information on remittance **inflows** reported to your institution varies by type of remittances services provider.

40. Please indicate whether remittance service providers in your country are:

a. Required to report each separate cross-border remittance **inflows** transaction	☐
b. Able to report multiple cross-border remittance **inflows** transactions periodically	☐
c. The answer depends on (varies by) the type of remittances service provider	☐

41. If you checked c. in Q. 40 above, would you please list the type(s) of remittance service providers in your country that are required to report each separate cross-border remittance **inflows** transaction.

42. If you checked b. or c. in Q. 40, would you please indicate how often remittance service providers in your country are required to make reports of multiple cross-border remittance **inflows** transactions:

a. Daily	☐
b. Weekly	☐
c. Monthly	☐
d. Quarterly	☐
e. Other: please specify	☐

43. Do the reporting requirements for cross-border remittance **inflows** transactions apply only at specific remittance thresholds (i.e., above a specified remittance amount)?

a. Yes	☐		b. No	☐

44. If yes to Q. 43, what is this threshold?

C. Reporting requirements for remittance outflows

45. Does your institution's statute or charter state explicitly that monitoring of remittance **outflows** is among your institution's functions?

a. Yes	☐	
b. No	☐	If you checked No at left, skip to Section III.D, Question 57

46. Are there reporting requirements with which institutions that send cross-border remittance **outflows** must comply?

a. Yes	☐	
b. No	☐	If you checked No at left, skip to Section III.D, Question 57

47. If yes, to Q. 46, please provide the following requested information in Table 11 on reporting requirements for each type of institution in your country that accepts remittances from senders in your country and sends these cross-border remittance **outflows** to beneficiaries abroad.

Table 11

	i. Please mark with an "X" if the institution is required to report remittance outflows to your institution	ii. Please list if there is another institution(s)/ government agency(ies) to which remittance outflows must be reported
a. Firms specialized in money transfers (Western Union, Money Gram, etc.)	☐	
b. Private commercial banks	☐	
c. State-owned banks	☐	
d. Exchange bureaus	☐	
e. Microfinance institutions	☐	
f. Savings and loan institutions	☐	
g. Credit unions and savings cooperatives	☐	
h. Other financial institutions that deliver remittances: please specify	☐	
i. Post offices	☐	
j. Mobile phone/telecoms service providers	☐	
k. Other non-financial institutions that deliver remittances: please specify	☐	

48. Please indicate below the specific types of information that must be reported by each type of institution that is required to report remittance **outflows** to your institution.

a. Remittance **outflows** transaction amounts	☐
b. Remittances "**destination country**" (that is, the country in which the remittances recipient is based)	☐
c. Specific instrument used to transmit remittances by senders in your country	☐
d. The mandatory information to be reported depends on (varies by) the type of remittances service provider	☐
e. Other: please specify	☐

49. If you checked d. in Q. 48 above, would you please specify how the type(s) of mandatory information on remittance **outflows** reported to your institution varies by type of remittances services provider.

50. Please indicate whether remittance service providers in your country are:

a. Required to report each separate cross-border remittance **outflows** transaction	☐
b. Are able to report multiple cross-border remittance **outflows** transactions periodically	☐
c. Options a. and b.: Answer depends on/varies by type of remittances service provider	☐

51. If you checked c. in Q. 50 above, would you please list the type(s) of remittance service providers in your country that are required to report each separate cross-border remittance **outflows** transaction.

52. If you checked b. or c. in Q. 50, would you please indicate how often remittance service providers in your country are required to make periodic reports to the relevant national authorities of multiple cross-border remittance **outflows** transactions:

a. Daily	☐
b. Weekly	☐
c. Monthly	☐
d. Quarterly	☐
e. Other: please specify	☐

53. Do the reporting requirements for cross-border remittance **outflows** transactions apply only at specific remittance thresholds (i.e., above a specified remittance amount)?

a. Yes	☐		b. No	☐

54. If yes to Q. 53, what is(are) the threshold amount(s)?

55. Have there been any recent or planned regulatory initiatives to seek to harmonize the reporting requirements with which cross-border remittance service providers in your country must comply?

a. Yes	☐		b. No	☐

56. If yes to Q. 55, would you please briefly describe those initiatives, the type(s) of remittance service providers to which these would apply, and the timing of these initiatives (i.e., specify dates of implementation if possible)?

D. National policies for anti-money laundering and combating the financing of terrorism

57. Is your institution involved in developing and/or implementing national policies for anti-money laundering and combating the financing of terrorism?

a. Yes	☐	
b. No	☐	If you checked No at left, skip to Section III.E, Question 65

58. What are the specific sanctions that are imposed in your country with regards to violations of regulations to prevent money laundering and to combat the financing of terrorism? Please check all that apply.

a. Fines for institutions and/or individuals who facilitate money laundering or the funding of terrorism	☐
b. Court-ordered freezing of funds involved in the particular transaction(s)	☐
c. Imprisonment	☐
d. Other: please specify	☐

59. Which entity(ies) in your countries enforce(s) these sanctions?

a. Central bank	☐
b. Ministry of finance	☐
c. A separate national (or regional) authority set up and specifically charged with preventing money laundering	☐
d. Other: please specify	☐

60. Is there a wing for anti-money laundering/combating the financing of terrorism within your country's general law enforcement authorities, which cooperates with your or other national authorities on compliance/enforcement matters?

a. Yes	☐		b. No	☐

61. Are there plans to enhance national regulations and mechanisms to prevent money laundering and to combat the financing of terrorism in your country?

a. Yes	☐		b. No	☐

62. If yes, to Q. 61, please describe these plans and envisaged date(s) for implementation.

63. Please provide the following further information in Table 12 on reporting requirements and associated documentation for each type of institution in your country that receives and/or sends cross-border remittance flows.

Table 12

	i. Are these remittance service providers obliged to file currency transaction reports? If yes, to which national authority?	ii. If yes to Q.i., is there an amount threshold for filing currency transaction reports? Please specify threshold	iii. Are there limits imposed on daily transaction amounts per customer? Please specify these limits	iv. Are these remittance service providers obliged to file suspicious activity reports? If yes, to which national authority?	v. If yes to Q.iv., is there an amount threshold for filing suspicious transaction reports? Please specify threshold
a. Firms specialized in money transfers (Western Union, Money Gram, etc.)					
b. Private commercial banks					
c. State-owned banks					
d. Exchange bureaus					
e. Microfinance institutions					
f. Savings and loan institutions					
g. Credit unions and savings cooperatives					
h. Other financial institutions that deliver remittances: please specify					
i. Post offices					
j. Mobile phone/telecoms service providers					
k. Other non-financial institutions that deliver remittances: please specify					

64. What additional regulations and mechanisms are currently in place to prevent money laundering and to combat the financing of terrorism in your country?

E. Foreign exchange regulations and related costs

65. Is your institution involved in developing and/or implementing national foreign exchange regulations?

a. Yes	☐	
b. No	☐	If you checked No at left, skip to Section IV, Question 82

66. Is it compulsory for recipients of remittance **inflows** in your country to convert the remittances into **local currency**?

a. Yes	☐		b. No	☐

67. Is there a ceiling that applies specifically for remittance **inflows** that are not converted into **local currency**?

a. Yes	☐		b. No	☐

68. If yes to Q. 67, what is this ceiling and the corresponding time period to which it applies?

69. Can people residing in your country send cross-border remittances (remittance **outflows**) denominated in **foreign currency** to recipients residing abroad?

a. Yes	☐		b. No	☐

70. Is there a remittance ceiling that applies specifically for remittance **outflows** that are denominated in **foreign currency**?

a. Yes	☐		b. No	☐

71. If yes to Q. 70, what is this ceiling and the corresponding time period to which it applies?

72. Can people residing in your country send cross-border remittances (remittance **outflows**) denominated in **local currency** to recipients residing abroad?

a. Yes	☐		b. No	☐

73. Is there a remittance ceiling that applies specifically for remittance **outflows** that are denominated in **local currency**?

a. Yes	☐		b. No	☐

74. If yes to Q. 73, what is this ceiling and the corresponding time period to which it applies?

75. Does the central bank have any legal powers to issue regulations to limit the costs related to the exchange rate to be used for remittance transactions?

| a. Yes ☐ | b. No ☐ |

76. If yes to Q. 75, has the central bank used these legal powers in order to lower currency conversion costs for remittances in the past five years?

| a. Yes ☐ | b. No ☐ |

77. If yes to Q. 75, how and when?

78. Does your country allow the general public to have deposit accounts in foreign currencies?

| a. Yes ☐ | b. No ☐ |

79. How do foreign exchange regulations related to cross-border remittance flows vary for different remittance service providers in your country? Please answer below for all applicable remittance service providers in your country.

Table 13

	i. Is this institution prohibited from handling foreign exchange transactions independently? Y/N	ii. Does the relevant regulatory authority place limits on this institution's amount of foreign exchange holdings or remittance inflows? Y/N	iii. Does the relevant regulatory authority place limits on this institution's remittance outflows? Y/N	iv. If yes to Q. ii and/or iii , what are these limits?
a. Firms specialized in money transfers (Western Union, Money Gram, etc.)				
b. Private commercial banks				
c. State-owned banks				
d. Exchange bureaus				
e. Microfinance institutions				
f. Savings and loan institutions				
g. Credit unions and savings cooperatives				
h. Other financial institutions that deliver remittances: please specify				
i. Post offices				
j. Mobile phone/telecoms service providers				
k. Other non-financial institutions that deliver remittances: please specify				

80. Does the central bank have any legal powers to issue regulations to limit the costs related to the transfer and/or sending of cross-border remittances?

a. Yes	☐		b. No	☐

81. If yes to Q. 80, has the central bank used these legal powers in order to lower these costs in the past five years?

a. Yes	☐	If you checked yes at left, how and when?
b. No	☐	

IV. Financial Infrastructure Supporting Cross-border Remittance Flows

This set of questions is intended to examine the extent to which current national financial infrastructure supports and facilitates cross-border remittance flows transmitted by all types of remittance service providers. This section is intended to take stock of recent and upcoming changes in national policy that would expand the access of various RSPs to financial infrastructure/systems and/or expand the outreach of remittance services to remote locations.

82. Please answer the questions in Table 14 about access to clearing and settlement systems by the remittance service providers in your country.

Table 14

	i. Has access to the central bank's clearing and settlement systems? Yes/No	ii. If applicable, are there plans to expand these institutions' access to these systems? Yes/No	iii. If applicable, what clearing and settlement systems do these institutions use?
a. Firms specialized in money transfers (Western Union, Money Gram, etc.)			
b. Private commercial banks			
c. State-owned banks			
d. Exchange bureaus			
e. Microfinance institutions			
f. Savings and loan institutions			
g. Credit unions and savings cooperatives			
h. Other financial institutions that deliver remittances: please specify			
i. Post offices			
j. Mobile phone/telecommunications service providers			
k. Other nonfinancial institutions that deliver remittances: please specify			

83. Are there any recent moves or plans to implement a common payment platform in your country and/or region, which would facilitate remittance transfers?

a. Yes	☐		b. No	☐

84. If yes to Q. 83, please describe these initiatives indicating implementation dates.

85. If yes to Q. 83, are/will all ATM and point of sale devices be linked/compatible with the common payment platform?

a. Yes	☐		b. No	☐

86. Have there been any initiatives by financial authorities to expand the outreach of remittances services to rural areas/remote locations in your country?

a. Yes	☐		b. No	☐

87. If yes to Q. 86, please briefly describe these initiatives, indicating implementation dates.

V. Best Practices, Public Policy Issues, Agreements for Data and Technology Sharing

By taking a cross country inventory of national authorities' views on best practices and important public policy issues, as well as the extent to which countries have negotiated data and/or technology sharing agreements to improve information and/or efficiency of systems, this set of questions seeks to gauge emerging priority policy issues and practices for the region and the extent to which countries make use of and benefit from collaborative agreements in this area.

88. From your perspective, are any of the following areas in need of improved policy coordination within your country? Please check all that apply.

a. Eliminating inconsistencies within national policy vis-à-vis remittance flows. Please specify	☐
b. Better management of the tension between improving financial access and avoiding financial crime.	☐
c. Other: please specify	☐

89. From your perspective, what are the areas that require more attention in order to make the transfer and delivery of remittances more efficient and secure? Please select all applicable areas.

a. Better statistics on remittances	☐
b. Better statistics and studies on migrants	☐
c. Increased competition among remittance service providers	☐
d. Delivery of remittances to remote areas	☐
e. New technologies and products for the provision of remittance services	☐
f. Financial integrity issues	☐
g. Other: please specify	☐

90. In your opinion, are there any practices that should be prohibited in order to make the transfer and delivery of cross-border remittances more secure?

91. Does your country restrict the sending of remittances to certain countries?

a. Yes	☐		b. No	☐

92. If applicable to which countries is the sending of remittances restricted?

93. Are there any formal or informal arrangements of which you are aware for data-sharing on cross-border remittance flows between institutions in your country and counterpart authorities in other countries?

a. Yes	☐	
b. No	☐	If you checked no at left, please skip to Q. 97

94. Would you please specify with which countries' national authorities your institution shares/exchanges data on cross-border remittance flows?

a)
b)
c)
d)

95. Would you please specify the type(s) of remittance data shared?

96. Please indicate below how often these data are exchanged.

a. Monthly	☐
b. Quarterly	☐
c. Annually	☐
d. Other; Please specify	☐

97. Are there any arrangements of which you are aware between national institutions and their counterparts in other countries that aim to improve the efficiency of cross-border remittance transmissions?

a. Yes	☐	
b. No	☐	If you checked no at left, please skip to Q. 100

98. Would you please specify with which countries' institutions these arrangements have been made?

a)
b)
c)
d)
e)

99. Would you please specify how these arrangements aim to improve the efficiency of cross-border remittance transmissions?

100. Is there any office in your country responsible for handling and resolving complaints of the clients of remittance service providers (that is, remittance recipients and/or senders) on issues related to the provision of cross-border remittance services?

a) Yes	☐		b) No	☐

101. If yes to Q. 100, what is the office?

102. If there is no such entity, how are those issues normally resolved?

103. What may be, in your opinion, inhibiting migrants residing in your country from using formal channels to transfer cross-border remittances to recipients abroad? Please check all that apply.

a. Sender's lack of valid identification	☐
b. No bank branch near residence of intended remittance beneficiary abroad	☐
c. Remittances sender's lack of access to bank accounts	☐
d. Mistrust of formal financial institutions	☐
e. Mistrust or lack of information about electronic transfers	☐
f. National payments systems' lack of capacity to transfer remittances quickly	☐
g. Foreign exchange controls	☐
h. High costs of services	☐
i. Remittance recipient country's tax policies on remittance inflows	☐
j. Your country's tax policies on remittance outflows	☐
k. Other: please specify	☐

104. In your opinion, what needs to be done in your country to encourage immigrants to transfer remittances to recipients abroad through formal channels? Please check all that apply.

a. Lift foreign exchange restrictions	☐
b. Allow remittance outflows to be denominated in any international currency and not just in local currency.	☐
c. Improve access to banking services of senders living in remote areas.	☐
d. Change senders'/public perception of formal financial institutions.	☐
e. Improve public awareness of innovative technologies available for remittance transfer.	☐
f. Improve postal service infrastructure to be able to deliver remittances to more locations	☐
g. Eliminate exclusivity contracts between money transfer operators and other institutions delivering remittances.	☐
h. Revise tax policies affecting remittances	☐
i. Other: please specify	☐

105. Are there any plans to foster the use of formal mechanisms to transfer remittances, instead of informal channels?

| a. Yes | ☐ | | b. No | ☐ |

106. If yes to Q. 105, please describe these initiatives:

Thank you for completing the survey and participating in our study.

Appendix 3. Geographical Distribution of Responses to Survey of Central Banks[1]

(as of December 2009)

Remittance-inflows questionnaire (version 1)

Sub-Saharan Africa		East Asia and Pacific	Europe and Central Asia	Latin America and Caribbean	Middle East and North Africa	South Asia	High-income countries
Botswana	Malawi	Fiji	Albania	Brazil	Algeria	Afghanistan	Barbados
Burkina Faso	Mali	Indonesia	Armenia	Chile	Lebanon	Bangladesh	Cyprus
Burundi	Mauritius	Philippines	Azerbaijan	Colombia	Morocco	India	Czech Republic
Cape Verde	Mozambique	Samoa	Belarus	El Salvador	Syria	Nepal	Poland
Congo, Rep. of	Namibia	Thailand	Bosnia and Herzegovina	Guatemala	Tunisia		Slovak Republic
Eritrea	Niger	Vanuatu	Bulgaria	Haiti			Slovenia
Ethiopia	Nigeria		Croatia	Honduras			
Gabon	Rwanda		Georgia	Jamaica			
Ghana	Senegal		Kyrgyz Republic	Mexico			
Guinea	Sierra Leone		Latvia	Nicaragua			
Guinea-Bissau	Swaziland		Lithuania	Paraguay			
Kenya	Tanzania		Moldova	Peru			
Lesotho	Uganda		Romania	Uruguay			
Madagascar	Zambia		Tajikistan				
			Turkey				

Remittance-outflows questionnaire (version 2)

High-income OECD		High-income, non-OECD countries	Developing countries
Australia	Italy	Aruba	Russian Federation
Austria	Japan	Bahamas	South Africa
Belgium	Luxembourg	Cayman Islands	Venezuela, R.B. de
Canada	Netherlands	Hong Kong, China	
Denmark	New Zealand	Israel	
Finland	Norway	Korea, Rep. of	
France	Portugal	Kuwait	
Germany	Spain	Macao, China	
Greece	Sweden	Oman	
Ireland	Switzerland	Qatar	
	United Kingdom	San Marino	

Note

[1] Covers the 112 country surveys that were submitted in sufficiently complete form for the purposes of the analysis undertaken in this paper.

Eco-Audit

Environmental Benefits Statement

The World Bank is committed to preserving Endangered Forests and natural resources. We print World Bank Working Papers and Country Studies on postconsumer recycled paper, processed chlorine free. The World Bank has formally agreed to follow the recommended standards for paper usage set by Green Press Initiative—a nonprofit program supporting publishers in using fiber that is not sourced from Endangered Forests. For more information, visit www.greenpressinitiative.org.

In 2008, the printing of these books on recycled paper saved the following:

Trees*	Solid Waste	Water	Net Greenhouse Gases	Total Energy
289	8,011	131,944	27,396	92 mil.
*40 feet in height and 6–8 inches in diameter	Pounds	Gallons	Pounds CO_2 Equivalent	BTUs